COMMODORE PERRY
AND THE OPENING OF JAPAN

COMMODORE PERRY AND THE OPENING OF JAPAN

---

by FERDINAND KUHN

Illustrated by J. GRAHAM KAYE

Landmark BOOKS

THIS SPECIAL EDITION IS PRINTED AND DISTRIBUTED BY
ARRANGEMENT WITH THE ORIGINATORS AND PUBLISHERS
OF LANDMARK BOOKS *Random House, Inc.,* NEW YORK, BY

E. M. HALE AND COMPANY
EAU CLAIRE, WISCONSIN

Contents

COMMODORE PERRY
AND THE OPENING OF JAPAN

I. Heading for the Unknown

Just over a hundred years ago, in the summer of 1853, four ships of the United States Navy sailed from China on a tricky and dangerous mission.

The sailors knew they were headed for a chain of islands marked on their maps as "Japan." But they didn't know what they would find when they got there, or whether they would ever come back alive.

Japan had been tightly closed to foreign ships and traders for more than two hundred years. Few outsiders had gone ashore there and lived to tell the tale.

The seamen on the four ships had heard blood-chilling stories of what the Japanese did to their prisoners. Aboard the steam frigate *Susquehanna,* the flagship of the squadron, the men grumbled as they swabbed the floor planks and polished the brass.

"I don't mind getting into a fair fight," one hard-bitten veteran complained to a neighbor on the deck. "But I hear they lock you in cages if you get captured —and I don't like the idea."

It was true. One shipwrecked American crew had been locked up like wild animals in a zoo, and the story had angered every Navy man who heard it.

"I don't see any sense in it," said the second seaman. "They've got thirty million people who would like to chop our heads off—and we've got only four ships. Look!"

He pointed beyond the stern of the *Susquehanna.* The flagship was pulling the sailing sloop *Saratoga* on a towrope. Across a few hundred yards of glassy water the steam frigate *Mississippi* was towing another sloop, the *Plymouth.*

These four ships were the entire squadron. On the wide, lonely expanse of the China Sea they looked as forlorn as four black beetles on a pond. Four ships were pitifully few, and the sailors knew it.

They might have faced the unknown more cheerfully if it had not been for the heat. The sun was scorching in that first week of July. The air hung heavy and oppressive, as in the calm before a summer cloudburst. In a day or two the squadron would be off the coast of Japan.

Suddenly, in the midday heat, the crew heard the drums announce, "Battle Stations!" At once the deck of the *Susquehanna* looked like a giant ant hill that someone had kicked with a boot.

Scores of white-clad sailors clambered up from below decks and raced to their fighting posts. Some of them, armed with pikes and cutlasses, crowded the rails, ready to repel an enemy attack. Marines standing behind them loaded their rifles and fired noiseless volleys.

Gun crews pulled in the big eight-inch guns, loaded them and rolled them out again so that they jutted beyond the gunwales.

Above the shouts of command and the clash of weapons being loaded, the sailors now heard the clanging of a bell. The bell meant that the ship was on fire. Sweating men rigged the pumps, unwound the hoses and pulled them into position to put out the flames. Finally the ship's band played "Yankee Doodle" as a signal that the enemy had been routed.

All this was a battle drill, not a real engagement. It had been part of the daily routine on every one of the four ships since the start of the expedition. These warships had to be ready for anything, even though their purpose was peaceful.

Their commander's assignment had seemed simple enough. It was to deliver a letter from the President of the United States, Millard Fillmore, to the Emperor of Japan.

But why did he need a squadron of warships to deliver a letter? Why couldn't the President have sent it by mail? Or why couldn't he have used the American ambassador in Japan as his messenger, as he did in other countries?

The answer, of course, is that in those days there was no mail service to Japan. There was no American ambassador there. There never had been any relations between the two governments or between their peoples.

Japan had banged and bolted her doors against the world long before there was any United States of America. Her rulers had chased out the missionaries, traders and other foreigners about the time the Pilgrims were landing in New England.

The only exceptions were a handful of Chinese and Dutch, who were allowed to keep a trading station on a little island in Nagasaki harbor, near the southern tip of Japan.

The rulers of Japan were afraid that European countries, especially Spain and Portugal, wanted to grab Japanese territory and make it a colony. They feared, too, that foreigners might stir up rebellions against their own rule inside Japan.

They shut their doors not only to keep foreigners out, but also to keep their own people in. Any Japanese who even tried to go abroad was almost sure to have his head cut off. It became a crime to build a ship big enough to sail from the Japanese islands to any foreign shore.

As a result, Japan had no ocean trade and no navy, although in the days of Columbus it had been a great seafaring nation. When the four American warships approached Japanese shores, the wall that Japan had built around herself was 216 years old, and few foreigners knew what was going on inside it.

The United States, in contrast, was "bustin' out all over" in the 1850's. It was like a big, brawny adolescent with boundless confidence in itself. Within North America, the young Republic was pushing west and southwest to bring vast new areas under the Stars and Stripes. Outside North America, Yankee clipper ships were sailing every sea and trading with every continent.

The closed islands of Japan had become a nuisance to the United States. Our ships in the China trade often needed coal, wood and water from Japan, and could not get it. They needed permission to shelter in quiet Japanese harbors during Pacific typhoons. Shipwrecked American seamen needed protection and a chance to return to their homes.

For these reasons the government in Washington fitted out an expedition to go to Japan. Its object was to persuade the Japanese rulers to make a treaty of trade and friendship.

The President and his advisers hoped the attempt would not lead to bloodshed. They insisted that the closed doors of Japan should be opened peacefully if possible. Fillmore ordered the commander of the expedition: "Make no use of force except in the last resort for defense, if attacked, and for self-preservation."

But nobody aboard the four ships knew what would happen. The ships were poking their noses into unfriendly territory, and maybe into a gigantic hornets' nest. Who could tell whether the Japanese would fight? And if they fought, who knew what cruelty, what cunning, what devilish devices they might use to drive the Americans away?

In subdued voices the seamen muttered against the Commodore of the expedition—"Old Matt," some of them called him. Most of them had never laid eyes on him, although he had commanded their little fleet ever since the ships had left Shanghai weeks before.

Few had a good word to say for him. The men were afraid he was leading them into a trap, to die for no good reason or to languish for years in cages.

They grumbled for still another reason. These blazing hot days in the China Sea were nothing but drill, drill, drill. For two years the crews of the *Susquehanna* had been on duty in Chinese waters, and those of the sloops even longer. They were tired and homesick, and blamed the Commodore for all their troubles.

Late in the afternoon of July 7th, when the seamen thought their day's work was done, they heard another roll of drums, then the beating of drums and another roll. This meant inspection at quarters.

Inspection again! After such a day? The Commodore must be out of his mind!

The men wiped the sweat from their faces, hustled into their uniforms and sullenly took their positions for inspection by their ship's captain. The red sun, low in the western sky, threw long shadows on the deck. It lit up the quarter-deck at the stern of the *Susquehanna*, the living quarters of the Commodore.

As the sailors lined up, some of them noticed a heavy-set man in a long blue coat and blue trousers, with a visored cap on his dark hair. He was standing at the stairway that led to his cabin, watching with a stern but satisfied expression on his face.

This was Commodore Matthew Calbraith Perry, the man on whom their fortunes now depended. This was the commander who was leading them toward dangerous shores.

2. Meet the Commodore

If you had been a sailor on one of Matthew Perry's ships, you might have feared him, but you would have respected him.

The name Perry was enough to command respect in the Navy. Matthew's father, four brothers and two brothers-in-law had been naval officers. One of his brothers was the dashing, charming Oliver Hazard

Perry, the hero of the Battle of Lake Erie in the War of 1812. It was Oliver who thrilled America with the report:

"We have met the enemy and they are ours!"

Matthew Perry was a contrast to Oliver in looks, in personality and in almost everything except personal courage. As he led his squadron toward Japan, he was almost sixty years old, proud and portly, blunt in speech and something of a terror to his men. An old seaman summed him up in this way:

"So long as ye walked a chalk line there couldn't be a fairer man than the Commodore—but God help ye if ye slipped over that line!"

His tongue lashings were long remembered. The sight of a smudge of dirt on deck would darken his face with anger. His thick black hair and eyebrows gave him the look of a shaggy dog—but not the kind you would ever pat or get familiar with.

It was dangerous for anyone of lower rank in the Navy to be familiar with Matthew Calbraith Perry, or to fail in the slightest degree to carry out his orders.

His officers and sailors thought he was as cold and unfeeling as a block of New England granite. They did not know the kindlier streaks in his nature. They did not know, for example, that this tough Yankee sailor had a soft spot in his heart for children. He had had ten children of his own. His pockets always bulged with presents when he came home from Navy duty.

But he didn't always understand children. Just before he sailed for Japan, Perry paid a good-bye visit to the family of his famous brother Oliver, who had died many years before. He asked his eight-year-old grand-nephew, Thomas Sergeant Perry:

"How would you like to come to Japan with me, Tom?"

The youngster disappeared like a shot. The Commodore had to go searching for him in the attic. He found the boy packing his belongings in an old sea chest, ready to go at once. The Commodore hadn't realized what hurt he had caused by making such an offer in fun.

Decades later Thomas did go to Japan after all. He stayed for three years as professor of English literature at Keio University in Tokyo.

Despite all his passion for discipline aboard his ships, Commodore Perry was not a bit old-fashioned in his ideas. He fought for changes and reforms in the Navy for most of his life.

As a young midshipman in the War of 1812—the youngest in the Navy when he was commissioned—he watched many floggings that bloodied the backs of seamen as punishments for trival offenses. He made up his mind that such brutality must stop. In 1851, the year before he sailed for Japan, he was a member of a government board that finally abolished flogging in the Navy.

Perry made and **enforced** strict rules to guard the

health of his men. He fought for better training of seamen and for the creation of the Naval Academy at Annapolis. Finally, Perry earned the title of "Father of the Steam Navy" by urging the use of steam power. Other old-timers in the Navy thought of steam as a new-fangled luxury. Perry saw it as a necessity, and won.

If the Commodore did so much for the Navy and its men, why was he not more popular? And why did otherwise loyal officers make fun of him behind his back?

One answer may be that Perry was vain. He took himself very, very seriously. He had a weakness for pomp and show, especially when he could be in the center of the stage. If he had not been born into a Navy family, with the salt of the sea in his nostrils, he could have been an actor in old-fashioned melodrama.

Perry also made enemies by taking his third son, Lieutenant Oliver Hazard Perry, as his secretary on his ship to Japan. Many other young officers had equally good records and were not chosen.

The government in Washington knew of Perry's weaknesses but felt that his good qualities were far more important. The leader of the Japan Expedition would have to be much more than a fighting man. He would have to be a diplomat who could bargain with foreigners without losing his temper. And he would have to be something of an explorer, since Japan in those days was a country virtually unknown.

Matthew Perry was the man for the job.

He set to work on his new assignment as if he were preparing to discover a new continent and fight a war at the same time. To learn what he could about Japan, he scoured New York and London for books, maps and charts. Before he sailed for Japan he had read forty books on the subject.

He hoped and guessed that his mission would find a place in history books. It might be the first meeting between two peoples who had never known each other. To make sure that there would be a complete record of the expedition, he took a famous young writer, Bayard Taylor, as one of his clerks.

He insisted on having official artists aboard his ships to paint the great event for future generations. He even took a photographer, the first ever assigned to a United States Government expedition. More far-sighted still was his decision to bring a farm expert to Japan. Perry foresaw that if his mission succeeded there could be a valuable exchange of ideas and skills, of seeds and farm tools, between the Americans and the Japanese.

What other naval officer of those days had so much imagination?

Long before Perry left the United States, he had a clear idea of how he was going to do the job in Japan. For one thing, he decided to impress the Japanese with all possible ceremony. As a young naval officer, on duty in the Baltic and the Mediterranean, he had dined with the czar of Russia, the king of France, the khedive of Egypt, the emperor of Austria and the bey of Tunis.

From watching these rulers and their glittering courts, he learned that pomp and formality were important in dealing with foreigners, especially with Easterners. Japan was no exception. Perry also resolved to succeed without using force—if he could avoid it. The commander of a naval squadron, he thought, did not need to open fire to get what he wanted from foreign rulers.

He remembered that in 1832 he had led a squadron to Naples to collect debts that were owed to American citizens. The king of Naples, a stubborn, dull-witted tyrant, was at least intelligent enough to understand the meaning of a gun when it was pointed at him.

Young Perry coolly ordered his ships into Naples harbor, one each day, until five ships were anchored with their guns trained on the royal palace. Not a shot was fired, but the king paid the debt. Congress was so pleased that it voted Perry $1,500 to repay him for his personal expenses on this errand.

If such a show of force worked wonders in Naples, wouldn't it do the same in Japan? Perry wondered.

He tried to discover why earlier American efforts to open Japan had failed. He thought of the brig *Morrison,* driven away by gunfire in 1837; of Commodore James Biddle, who let himself be pushed back into his boat when he tried to land in 1846; of Commander Glynn, in the *Preble,* who rescued fourteen American castaways in 1849 but failed to pry Japan open to Western trade.

What was wrong with all these attempts? Perry thought he knew the answer. The earlier American naval men did not have enough ships and guns to compel Japanese respect. They did not know enough about the Japanese mentality to get what they wanted without shooting.

Commodore Perry was going to be different.

He persuaded the government in Washington to let him have a truly imposing squadron. The Navy Department promised him five paddle-wheeled steamers and seven sailing ships. This was a promise the government did not keep. When Perry reached China, he found only four ships at his disposal for the first visit to Japan.

Now he was almost within sight of the dreaded Japanese coast. His squadron was far too small for safety. His own wits, his tact and firmness, would have to make up for the warships he did not have. In a day or two he might learn whether his ideas and his plans were right.

3. Into Forbidden Waters

Soon after sunrise on the morning of July 8, 1853, the steep mountain sides of the Japanese coast loomed up through the morning mist. The first land sighted was Cape Idzu, forty miles from the narrow entrance of what is now called Tokyo Bay.

As a bright summer sun pierced the fog, the Americans could see a coastline as green as the shores of Ireland. Far in the distance, seeming to float above the sea and the land, the white cone of Mount Fuji pointed to the sky.

The familiar order "Battle Stations!" beat from the drums of the flagship *Susquehanna,* and was flagged to the other three vessels of the squadron. An added order came from the Commodore. To guard against a Japanese attack, he signaled:

"Have no communication with shore! Allow none from shore!"

This was no rehearsal. The squadron was in forbidden waters. It was on the alert for trouble.

Two Japanese fishing boats, passing near, shifted course and steered back toward shore as if to bring news that foreign warships were approaching. The American ships steamed straight on, with sails furled, into a head wind.

The great paddle wheels thrashed round and round, in unbroken rhythm, pushing the steamers forward at eight or nine knots. The two sailing sloops followed at the ends of their towropes.

Seen through Japanese eyes of that day, Perry's black steamers were evil monsters from another world. They vomited black smoke. They moved into the wind—"like arrows," the Japanese said—without sail or oars. They plowed, with bold indifference, into waters that had been closed to foreigners for 216 years.

The crew of one Japanese sailboat were so terri-

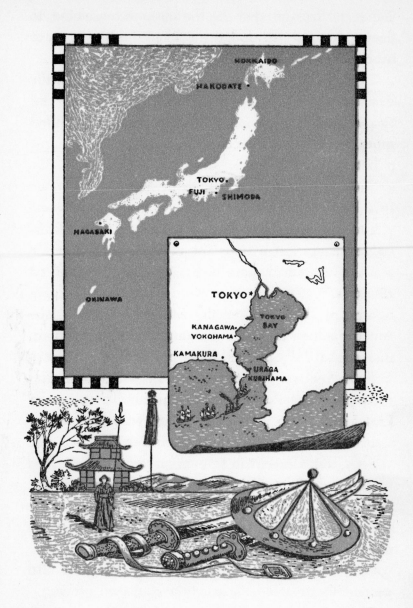

fied that they dropped their square sails and began rowing furiously to dodge the black hulls that were bearing down upon them.

Off the western entrance to Tokyo Bay, the squadron stopped while the captains were rowed to the *Susquehanna* for a final briefing by Perry. Soon they were facing the Commodore in his cabin.

"Sit down, gentlemen," the Commodore began. He was always courteous on such occasions.

"I have asked you to come because I now want you to hear the instructions I have had from Washington. These instructions are as much for you as for me. I want you to remember them carefully, and at all times."

Perry walked over to the safe in his cabin and pulled out two important-looking documents. Slowly and emphatically he read these passages of his orders from the Secretary of State:

"Commodore Perry will bear in mind that, as the President has no power to declare war, his mission is necessarily of a peaceful character. He will not resort to force except in self-defense.

"In his dealings with the Japanese people, who are said to be proud and vindictive in character, he should be courteous and conciliatory, but at the same time firm and decided."

Perry looked up from his reading and said he wanted to stress one instruction above all others:

"Do everything to impress the Japanese with a just sense of the power and greatness of this country."

"Is that understood?" the Commodore asked. The captains nodded assent. Perry did not tell them that he had written most of the instructions himself, at the request of the Secretary of State.

The Secretary of the Navy had also given orders, which Perry now read. The expedition was to survey Tokyo Bay, make careful notes, draw sketches and maps where possible, and collect every scrap of information that might be useful to the government in Washington.

"Today," said the Commodore gravely, "we anchor in Tokyo Bay. Nobody knows what will happen. I want every man on your ships to show the utmost caution and vigilance."

Perry knew each of these captains personally. He had chosen them for the Japan Expedition because he had confidence in their good sense as well as in their courage. He thanked them for coming and sent them back to their ships.

"Good luck to you all!" he called after them.

The engines started again and the ships steamed to within two miles of the shore. As they neared the uncharted coast, the ships reduced speed. The American sailors were close enough to see a large town lying beneath the green bluffs of the shoreline.

A fleet of more than a dozen small boats pushed

off from shore. They were heavily manned, and flew banners with big Japanese characters painted on them, as if to show that they had officials aboard. The squadron steamed relentlessly ahead and left the Japanese far behind.

Late in the afternoon, the squadron stood off Uraga, a city of about 20,000 within a cove on the western side of Tokyo Bay. Now the Americans were only thirty-five miles from the city of Tokyo (called Yedo in those days)—closer than foreign ships had come to the capital of Japan in more than two hundred years.

The crews were watchful. When the ships were a mile and a half inside the bay, two loud gunshots split the air and echoed against the hilly shore.

A puff of smoke high above the coast told the Americans that a fort had signaled—either to announce their arrival or to warn them not to come nearer.

4. Perry Wins the First Round

If the shots were a warning, Perry took no notice of it. The warships groped forward, sounding the depth of the bay almost yard by yard. Then Perry ordered the towropes cast off. The four ships began forming a line so that a broadside from their guns could command Uraga and its harbor.

Before the clumsy paddle wheels had stopped turning, a swarm of rowboats shot out from the shore like so many bees escaping from a hive. In each boat about thirty men stood at their oars like Venetian gondoliers. The boats, too, were like gondolas, with sharp bows and slightly tapering sterns.

The men in these boats—the first Japanese Perry's sailors had seen—were tall and muscular. They were stripped to the waist, and their backs shone in the late afternoon sun. The crowns of their heads were shaved except for a topknot. A few wore shiny lacquer helmets painted with coats of arms, which probably marked them as officials.

Each of the little boats flew from its stern the horizontally striped flag of the Japanese ruler: white, black and white.

When the *Plymouth* blew her whistle, with a screeching blast, the entire crew of one of the Japanese boats dived overboard in panic. Aboard one of the other boats a wrinkled official, wearing two swords and a flowing gown, held up a scroll with French words on it. It warned the Americans to go away, and indicated that they should anchor only at their peril.

The boat nosed alongside, and the old official grabbed the side of the flagship where the bow railing had been lowered.

"Don't let him aboard!" was the order. A sentry poked a musket in his face, and a line of pikes at the sides of the ship persuaded him to let go. At this moment another of the Japanese spoke up, in faultless English:

"I can speak Dutch!"

This explained a great deal to Perry and his officers. A few Japanese officials had picked up the Dutch language at the trading post which the Hollanders had been allowed to keep in Nagasaki harbor. The fact that a Dutch-speaking interpreter had been brought to Tokyo Bay from Nagasaki, 500 miles away, showed that the Japanese had expected the Americans. Spies in the Ryukyu Islands, on Perry's route, had told them that the squadron was bound for Uraga.

Now the Commodore's Dutch-speaking interpreter, Portman, went into action. The Japanese interpreter began firing a volley of questions.

"Do these ships come from America?" he asked— indicating again that he knew whose ships were coming.

"Yes," was the answer.

"You must allow me on board," the Japanese demanded.

"No, sir," said Portman. "The commander of this squadron is of the highest rank in the American Navy. He will only meet someone of the highest rank at Uraga."

"But I have the vice-governor of Uraga in my boat. He has the highest position in the city, and he is the proper person to be received."

"Why only a vice-governor?" Portman wanted to know. "Why didn't the governor himself come?"

"Because," the Japanese answered, with hot temper in his eyes and manner, "our laws forbid the governor from going aboard ships in the bay."

Finally Perry agreed to appoint an officer of the second rank to meet with the vice-governor. The Commodore himself would stay out of sight. The Japanese must understand that he would not demean himself by talking to men of lesser rank. To carry on the discussions with the Japanese, he appointed Lieutenant Contee, his flag lieutenant.

"Now tell me, please, why have you come?" the vice-governor began.

"The Commodore has been sent here on a friendly mission," was Contee's answer, translated into Dutch and then into Japanese. "He has brought a letter from the President of the United States to your Emperor. He would like to have an official of suitable rank sent aboard to get a copy of the letter. Then the Commodore would like to set a day for him to deliver the original on shore."

"Impossible!" the peppery vice-governor snapped back. "The laws of Japan state clearly that Nagasaki is the only place where we can do business with foreigners. Your ships will have to go there."

"We are not going to Nagasaki," the flag lieutenant said quietly. "The Commodore came here purposely because this place is near your capital. His intentions are friendly, and he expects the letter to be received here."

At this point a deck officer reported to Contee that the little Japanese guard boats were forming a ring around the entire squadron. Their crews were putting on long robes to keep warm. The boats contained sleeping mats, water and blankets, as if the oarsmen had come for a long stay.

"What shall we do, sir?"

The flag lieutenant hurried into Perry's cabin for new instructions. When he emerged he talked sternly to the Japanese visitors.

"We insist," he said, "that none of your boats shall hang around our ships to watch them. Why are they forming a ring around us?"

"It is Japanese custom and Japanese law," was the answer, "and we must carry them out."

"Well, sir," said Contee, "we Americans have our customs too. One of our laws is that no boat can come within a certain range of a man-of-war."

"What are the names of your ships?" the Japanese persisted. "How many men have you, and how many guns?"

"Our custom is never to answer such questions," Contee said sharply. He demanded again that the Japanese boats go away.

"We shall be sorry, with our kind and friendly feelings toward you, to do you any harm or to come into any collision with you," Contee went on, echoing the Commodore's orders. "But if you do not order your boats off, we shall fire into them and drive them off."

The vice-governor did not need further persuasion. He hurried to the gangway and gave an order which sent most of the boats scuttling back to the shore. A few lingered on, but were chased away by a boat from the *Susquehanna*. No more was seen of them during the squadron's entire stay. Soon the vice-governor left, saying that an officer of higher rank would come from Uraga in the morning.

The Commodore was pleased. He had accomplished three important things on his first day in Japanese waters. First, he had refused to go to Nagasaki, where American castaways had been caged and otherwise mistreated. Second, he had dealt firmly with the nuisance of the guard boats. Finally, he had impressed upon the rank-conscious Japanese that he would deal only with officials of the highest rank.

Down in the wardroom of the *Mississippi,* young William H. Rutherford, the assistant engineer, started a long letter in tiny, precise handwriting to Sarah Baldwin, his sweetheart in Philadelphia.

"The course which Commodore Perry has taken in this affair has astonished us all," he wrote. "He is very independent and says that no one shall take the letter to the Emperor unless he is of a rank with himself."

But Rutherford was still fearful. "It is my opinion," he wrote, "that if we do undertake to go up and anchor off the city of Tokyo we certainly will have a hard time of it. The Japanese are so thickly inhabited that they could devour us all in fifty minutes."

And Contee, who had conducted the day's dealings with the Japanese, wrote his wife:

"We lie down tonight in the neighborhood of ten million men, brave, enterprising, ready, never conquered. It behooves us to be watchful."

As darkness settled on the bay, Perry ordered the sentries doubled to keep intruders off. Steam was kept in the boilers. Muskets were stacked on the quarterdeck, and the boats were stored with carbines, pistols, cutlasses, and laudanum (opium) to dull the pain of the wounded if there should be a fight.

But the waters off Uraga were as quiet as a pond. Now and then a coastal ship glided past, its lanterns twinkling. The American sailors could see beacon fires glowing on every hilltop and lanterns swaying from the guard boats moored along the shore. From far away, they heard the deep tolling of a bell.

The nine-o'clock gun of the *Susquehanna* echoed back and forth and apparently spread alarm on shore. The fires went out.

Late that night the sentries saw a meteor shoot across the sky. It lit up the spars, sails and hulls of the American ships with a bluish light. Trailing sparks, it arched and fell slowly into the sea.

Perry took it as a sign of good luck. "The ancients," he wrote, "would have construed this as a favorable omen for any enterprise they had undertaken. It may be so construed by us, as we pray God that our present attempt, to bring a singular and isolated people into the family of civilized nations, may succeed without bloodshed."

5. Trickery and Tension

Early the next morning the American sentries saw two official boats pulling up to the *Susquehanna*. At a safe distance another boatload of Japanese had been sketching the American warships since sunrise.

"We have the Governor of Uraga aboard," a Dutch-speaking interpreter shouted from one of the visiting boats. The old Commodore was getting results!

Yesterday the laws of Japan had forbidden the Governor to board the ships in the bay. Now, and the Commodore chuckled, his firmness had brought the Governor himself.

Perry assigned two of his highest officers and his personal aide to greet the official visitor at the head of the ship's ladder. The Commodore stayed secluded in his cabin, which his men jokingly called the "forbidden interior." He would not deal with a mere governor.

To the Americans, however, the Governor looked as magnificent as a prince or an emperor. His long robe of rich brocade was embroidered with a peacock feather pattern. The robe was bordered in silver and gold, indicating that he was a noble of the third rank.

Though Perry and his officers did not suspect it, he was not a nobleman at all, but only the chief of police at Uraga. The Japanese had given him the robes and title of "Governor" for the purpose of dealing with the despised foreigners. No real Japanese nobleman would have lowered himself by doing business with "barbarians," regardless of their rank.

The Governor was introduced as "Kayama Yezaemon, the most important personage in Uraga." (In Japan last names come first and given names last. Kayama was his last name.) The discussion with Perry's officers began badly.

"What we want to know, sir," the Americans persisted, "is when we may deliver the letter from our President on shore. And we expect a high-ranking representative of your Emperor to receive it."

"It will take four days to get an answer from Tokyo," the so-called Governor answered.

"No," the Americans said, remembering that Tokyo was within an hour's steaming up the bay from the anchorage. "We expect an answer in three days. If not, our Admiral"—they meant, of course, the Commodore—"will go ashore with a big enough force of men to deliver it in person, no matter what the consequences may be.

"And by the way"—the American interpreter turned to the Japanese interpreter—"when you refer to the President of the United States you will please use the same language of respect as if you were speaking of your Emperor." Those were Perry's instructions.

With much ceremonial bowing, but without answering the American requests, the Governor left for shore to consult his superiors. The Commodore was ready to wait three days and no longer.

During the long wait Perry ordered a survey boat from each of his four warships to row up the bay toward Tokyo each morning. He wanted them to sound the depth of the water and to map the unknown shores. Each boat flew a white flag at its bow as a sign of peaceful intentions, but each was fully manned and armed to guard against an attack from the Japanese.

Sometimes the surveying parties rowed close enough to the shore to see primitive hillside fortifications of wood and mud, which would have been easy targets for the American guns. Lines of Japanese soldiers, bristling with pikes and old-fashioned matchlock rifles, stood in front of these forts.

But they were not so dangerous as they looked. When one of the American officers leveled a spyglass at them from a hundred yards off shore, the Japanese soldiers thought he was aiming a gun. They scurried out of sight, although they probably outnumbered the Americans a hundred to one. A Japanese boat tried to pursue the American surveyors, but the American crewmen dropped their oars, grabbed their carbines and stood as if ready to shoot. The Japanese boat made no further trouble.

One of the waiting days was Sunday, the first Sabbath day since the squadron had arrived in Japan. On the long voyage the Commodore had sometimes neglected Sunday services on shipboard, especially when it was cold or stormy. This time he decided to hold a full-dress service. He planned it knowing that no Christian worship had been permitted in Japan for almost 250 years.

So, on Sunday morning, the Japanese crowding the shoreline saw more than three hundred of the

Americans, in spick-and-span blue and white uniforms,
standing in ordered ranks on the deck of the *Susquehanna*. The chaplain read the Scriptures in a deep
ringing voice that could be heard far out across the
bay. The band played the swelling harmonies of familiar hymns, and three hundred sailors joined in
singing "Old Hundred."

On Monday, the third day of waiting for the Japanese answer, a survey boat from the *Mississippi*
pushed through the narrow inner entrance to Tokyo
Bay, where the shorelines make an hourglass pattern.

More than a thousand Japanese soldiers on the
eastern shore swarmed to the water's edge. Scores
of high-prowed guard boats darted out into the bay
to turn the Americans back. Behind the American
boat the great hulk of the *Mississippi* followed up the
bay, keeping the surveying party always within
range of its protecting guns.

As thirty-five Japanese boats closed in around him,
Lieutenant Silas Bent, in command of the American
survey group, ordered his men to stop rowing and
fix bayonets. Cold steel flashed in the sun. Answering flashes from the boats and the shore showed that
the Japanese had unsheathed their sharp swords.

Both groups stood for a few moments, tense, ready
for action, expecting shots at any moment.

6. A Threat Pays Off

For the first time the squadron was dangerously close to a bloody clash. It was a moment for iron nerve and self-control.

Lieutenant Bent remembered the Commodore's order not to fight unless attacked. He turned back to the sheltering guns of the *Mississippi*, feeling that his sally into the upper bay had been worth-while.

His surveying party had done a useful job of sounding and charting new areas of Tokyo Bay.

More important, the advance of the *Mississippi*, never far behind him, had served as a threat. The Commodore thought he might prod the Japanese into quicker answers if he sent one of his black ships up the bay toward their capital.

Perry was right. The *Mississippi* had hardly dropped anchor in its old position when the Governor's boat pulled alongside once more. Kayama, now deeply troubled, hurried aboard and bowed, grasping his knees and bending his head low in Japanese fashion.

"I think the answer from Tokyo will arrive tomorrow," he told Perry's interpreters. "But by the way, why did your ship and the survey boat go so far up the bay?"

Perry had an answer ready.

"The reason, sir," said the American interpreter, "is that the Commodore will have to return next spring with a larger force if our business is not settled on this visit. And if he comes next spring he will want a safer anchorage near Tokyo."

This added threat had its intended effect. Kayama had seen how easy it was for the big warship to steam almost within cannon range of the flimsy wooden houses of Tokyo. He left, with the usual ceremonial bows, and the next day came back with the answer. A high official would be ready to receive the President's letter on shore "the day after tomorrow," July 14th.

Now that the Americans had got what they wanted, and without bloodshed, they set out to show their good will toward Kayama and his two Japanese interpreters. Whether their guest was a real or a sham governor, the Americans found that he had good manners and a sense of humor.

They first brought out whisky, brandy and sweet liqueurs. Kayama smacked his lips and drained his glass down to the last drop. His Japanese companions watched him with mock alarm. They told the Americans, laughing, that they were afraid the Governor would take a drop too much.

"His face," they said, "is already growing red."

Kayama threw formality overboard. He cracked Japanese jokes, which had to be translated first into Dutch and then into English. And he quickly showed the Americans that he was an educated man who knew more about the Western world than they had imagined.

When the Americans showed him a globe, he put his fingers on Washington and New York, and said one was the capital and the other the commercial center of the United States. He identified Boston, Philadelphia and New Orleans.

"This is England," he said, locating the British Isles, "this France, this Denmark." He pointed to Mexico and said the United States now had a part

of it—probably a reference to the annexations that
had followed the Mexican War only a few years
before. Perry's officers were still more amazed when
Kayama asked:

"Don't you have roads cut through your mountains in the United States?"

The Americans guessed that he had heard about
the tunnels on American railroads, most of which
were less than twenty years old.

"And is the canal across the isthmus finished?"
he asked, pointing to the narrow strip on the map
connecting North and South America. The Americans
assumed that he meant the railroad then being built
across Panama. The canal was still more than fifty
years in the future, and was not even planned in
Perry's day.

Perry's spokesman then showed Kayama over the
ship—except the "forbidden interior" where the Commodore still hid himself from Japanese eyes. Crowds
of sailors gaped at the Japanese visitors, but Kayama
and his interpreters kept a grave dignity, as if they
had been among American sailors all their lives.

They saw the big gun and named it, correctly, the
"Paixhan." They climbed down into the engine room
and seemed to know the principles of steam locomo-
tion. Weren't such engines also used for transportation on American roads? they asked. Nothing seemed
to surprise these intelligent Japanese.

Another day of haggling was needed to arrange

the ceremony of receiving the President's letter. The Commodore was worried about one aspect of the landing. The Japanese wanted it to take place two miles down the bay, at a spot that could not be seen from the squadron's anchorage. Suppose these Japanese were planning treachery: how could the Americans forestall it if their warships were two miles away?

While his officers were talking to Kayama in the next cabin, the watchful Commodore took a necessary precaution. He ordered a survey boat to go down the bay to the proposed landing place to see whether the water was deep enough for American warships to anchor offshore. He was anxious that the big guns of both the *Susquehanna* and the *Mississippi* should cover both the landing and the ceremony. The survey launch rowed silently down the bay. Perry's officers kept Kayama busy talking.

Meanwhile the American surveyors found the landing place to be a gently curving beach to the right of the little town of Kurihama. An army of Japanese workers was busy putting up a wooden building for the ceremony. Coolies were carrying furniture on their backs into the building. Most important for Perry's purposes, the water was found to be deep enough for the big steamers to anchor.

The launch returned as silently as it had gone, and its commanding officer reported to Perry. Word went in to the officers who were talking to Kayama.

Soon they ushered the Governor off the ship with the usual politeness on both sides. The Japanese-Dutch interpreter had learned enough English to say distinctly to his American hosts, "Want to go home!"

Now, with businesslike decision, Perry called the captains of his four ships for another meeting in his cabin.

"Gentlemen," he said briskly, "we are going to move all the ships early in the morning to an anchorage off Kurihama. We shall anchor in line, covering the whole bay. I do not know why the Japanese chose this meeting place, but I want to be ready for anything.

"I know that all hands will want to go ashore, but we shall have to leave enough on board to do ships' duty. Perhaps the fairest thing will be to draw lots for the officers and men who go ashore.

"The ships will watch the proceedings on shore. They will have their guns primed and pointed, and their remaining boats alongside will have arms in them. The boats will be ready to shove ashore if the commanding officers think they are needed.

"I want all the officers who can possibly leave the ships to be ready in full uniform. They are to come to the reception with me, because I want the group with me to be as imposing as we can make it.

"The boats that carry the men ashore are all to have anchors," the Commodore went on. As if he had an afterthought, Perry ordered that the small boats should have bread and water in them in the event of being cut off from the warships. As usual he was leaving nothing to chance.

The four ships' captains left to give instructions to their crews. It would be a busy night for them, and a busier morning. If all went well, they would be the first Americans to set foot peacefully on the soil of the forbidden Empire. If it turned out to be an ambush—

Major Zeilin, the fine old fighting man who commanded Perry's marines, summed up the general feeling to a friend on the *Mississippi:*

"No cages tomorrow; it will be a fight to the death!"

7. The Magnificent Landing

As the American warships rounded the headland early on the morning of July 14, 1853, the seamen wondered:

Were they sailing into the pages of a story book or walking into a trap?

The crescent beach at Kurihama was bright with flags and uniforms that might have come straight out of the days of knights and chivalry. Scarlet pennons flapped from nine huge poles set up in the sand. Canvas screens stretched almost to the ends of the beach. They were decorated with the symbols of the Emperor of Japan.

The paddle wheels splashed, the ships glided across a mirror-like bay. Soon the sailors on board could see thousands of soldiers drawn up at the edge of the beach. The American officers, looking through their spyglasses, did not fail to notice that the Japanese were fully armed. Some wore long swords that gleamed in the morning light.

The Americans also noticed a building with conical towers, standing in the middle of the row of tall poles. This, apparently, was where the Commodore was expected to deliver the letter from the President to the Emperor.

The warships anchored as close to the shore as possible, with a loud clanking of their anchor chains. Little launches and cutters clustered alongside to take the first Americans ashore. The sailors wore natty blue trousers, white shirts and hats with thirteen stars on them, and carried rifles with bayonets fixed. The marines were in full-dress blue uniforms, with white straps crossed on their chests. The officers wore plain blue jackets and trousers, an "undress" uniform which they had worn on the Commodore's orders.

Perry had decked himself with every scrap of

gold braid in his wardrobe. If the Japanese were making this a big occasion—and the scene on the shore made it clear that they were—he was not going to let them outshine him.

Although it was a day of blazing heat, the Commodore had struggled into his heavy full-dress uniform. He buttoned his stiff gold collar tight around his neck; he put on all his medals and ribbons. While his officers and men were embarking for the landing, the Commodore sat in front of a mirror smoothing his wavy black hair. Lastly he set his cocked hat, dazzling with gold braid, on top of his big head.

He was ready to meet the representative of the Emperor on equal terms.

The first American rowboats skimmed toward the temporary landing place of sandbags and straw that had been built out into the gently lapping waves. Sailors and marines leaped ashore, armed to the teeth with swords, revolvers and cutlasses. Quickly they formed into double lines on either side of the landing place and stood stiffly waiting for the Commodore to arrive. Soon they could hear the tootling of the ships' bands as they were rowed to the beach for the ceremony.

A salute of thirteen guns boomed from the *Susquehanna* to announce that the Commodore was coming. The sailors and marines presented arms. The Commodore, with the slow majesty of an emperor, stepped ashore—the first foreign ambassador to set

As the bands blared, a parade of marines and sailors

formed to escort the Commodore to the reception house

foot on Japanese soil since the foreigners were expelled more than two hundred years before.

"Hail, Columbia! Happy Land!"

The combined ships' bands crashed into the rousing rhythms of what was then the nearest to an official anthem of the United States. Somehow it expressed better than any other song the pride that filled Perry's men on the landing day.

As the bands blared, a parade formed to escort the Commodore to the reception house: first the marines, then the sailors, then two ship's boys carrying a mysterious-looking scarlet velvet case. Inside it were two boxes. One contained President Fillmore's letter to the Emperor, the other the Commodore's credentials, the proof that he really was the President's representative.

Ahead of the Commodore marched two flag bearers, the tallest and heftiest men who could have been found on the squadron. On either side of him walked two tall Negro seamen as a personal guard.

As the parade crunched up the sandy beach, the band switched into lilting strains of "Don't You Remember Sweet Alice, Ben Bolt?"—a popular ballad of the period which was also a jaunty marching song. Instead of making a beeline for the reception house, the parade swung around in a half-circle so that all 112 marines, the 120 seamen, the 50 officers and 40 bandsmen could make a show of strength. In addi-

tion to the Japanese soldiers, thousands of villagers
and farmers from Kurihama were peeping from behind the canvas screens.

The Commodore entered a huge vestibule tent
about forty feet square. On the canvas roof was the
Emperor's coat of arms. Across the white canvas floor
a strip of red carpeting led to a single step and a
raised room beyond. The inner room was carpeted
in red. Over the rough timbers hung purple cloth
with white decorations. As the Commodore walked
in, he saw on his right a row of armchairs for himself
and his officers; on his left was a row of low stools beside which stood two Japanese in rich silk robes.

They bowed solemnly to the Commodore. The interpreter introduced one as "The Prince of Idzu";
the other, at least fifteen years older, with a wrinkled
face, was presented as "The Prince of Iwami." Perry
took these to be genuine princes sent by the Emperor.
He was wrong.

The Japanese were playing the same trick they
had used in introducing Kayama as "Governor" of
Uraga. The "Prince of Idzu" was not a prince at all,
but was really the governor of Uraga. The "Prince
of Iwami" was nothing but a government censor in
Tokyo.

Perry could not have known of this deception, and
probably it did not matter. For there was no doubt,
from the elaborate arrangements made by the Jap-

anese, that the two "princes," whatever their rank
and title, were really representatives of the ruler of
Japan.

At the head of the room, facing Perry as he entered,
stood a big red box of lacquer with feet of brass.
Kayama, the so-called Governor, and his Japanese
interpreter knelt beside it. Kayama asked:

"Are the letters ready to be delivered? The Prince
is ready to receive them, and this box is the place to
put them."

Perry motioned to the two ship's boys. They
brought the velvet case forward. The Commodore's
towering Negro guards opened it, took out the two
boxes containing the letters, held them up for all to
see and then placed them on the lid of the scarlet
box.

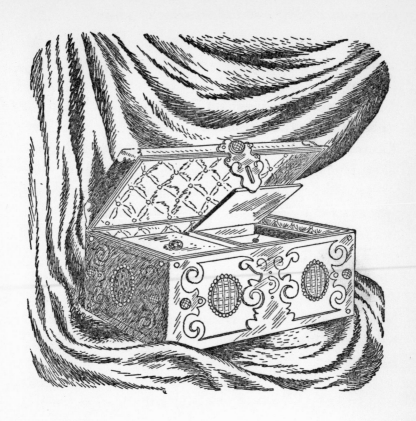

8. "Great and Good Friend!"

The box that held President Fillmore's letter to the Emperor had cost $1,000 to make. It was of rosewood, lined with blue velvet and held together with pure gold hinges, clasps and clamps.

The letter is worth reading today because it gives the best explanation of why Perry was sent to Japan. It also shows clearly the spirit in which the United

States was asking Japan to open its doors to friendship and trade.

President Fillmore began with the salutation "Great and Good Friend!" This did not mean, of course, that the President knew the Emperor personally. No foreigner did, and only a few high-ranking Japanese had ever laid eyes on this half-divine personage. "Great and Good Friend" was simply the form used by the head of one nation in writing to the head of another.

This is the Fillmore letter:

"I send you this public letter by Commodore Matthew C. Perry, an officer of the highest rank in the Navy of the United States, and commander of the squadron now visiting your imperial majesty's dominions.

"I have directed Commodore Perry to assure your imperial majesty that I entertain the kindest feelings toward your majesty's person and government, and that I have no other object in sending him to Japan but to propose to your imperial majesty that the United States and Japan should live in friendship and have commercial intercourse with each other.

"The Constitution and laws of the United States forbid all interference with the religious or political concerns of other nations. I have particularly charged Commodore Perry to abstain from every act which could possibly disturb the tranquility of your imperial majesty's dominions.

"The United States of America reach from ocean to ocean, and our Territory of Oregon and State of California lie directly opposite to the dominions of your imperial majesty. Our steamships can go from California to Japan in eighteen days.

"Our great State of California produces about sixty millions of dollars in gold every year, besides silver, quicksilver, precious stones and many other valuable articles. Japan is also a rich and fertile country, and produces many very valuable articles. Your imperial majesty's subjects are skilled in many of the arts. I am desirous that our two countries should trade with each other, for the benefit both of Japan and the United States.

"We know that the ancient laws of your imperial majesty's government do not allow of foreign trade, except with the Chinese and the Dutch; but as the state of the world changes and new governments are formed, it seems to be wise, from time to time, to make new laws. There was a time when the ancient laws of your imperial majesty's government were first made.

"About the same time America, which is sometimes called the New World, was first discovered and settled by the Europeans. For a long time there were but a few people, and they were poor. They have now become quite numerous; their commerce is very extensive; and they think that if your imperial majesty were so far to change the ancient laws as to allow a free trade between the two countries it would be extremely beneficial to both.

"If your imperial majesty is not satisfied that it would be safe altogether to abrogate [cancel] the ancient laws which forbid foreign trade, they might be suspended for five or ten years, so as to try the experiment. If it does not prove as beneficial as was hoped, the ancient laws can be restored. The United States often limit their treaties with foreign States to a few years, and then renew them or not, as they please.

"I have directed Commodore Perry to mention another thing to your imperial majesty. Many of our ships pass every year from California to China; and great numbers of our people pursue the whale fishery near the shores of Japan. It sometimes happens, in stormy weather, that one of our ships is wrecked on your imperial majesty's shores. In all such cases we ask, and expect, that our unfortunate people should be treated with kindness, and that their property should be protected, till we can send a vessel and bring them away. We are very much in earnest in this.

"Commodore Perry is also directed by me to represent to your imperial majesty that we understand there is a great abundance of coal and provisions in the Empire of Japan. Our steamships, in crossing the great ocean, burn a great deal of coal, and it is not convenient to bring it all the way from America. We wish that our steamships and other vessels should be allowed to stop in Japan and supply themselves with coal, provisions, and water. They will pay for them in money, or anything else your imperial majesty's subjects may prefer; and we request your imperial majesty to appoint a convenient port, in the southern part of the Empire, where our vessels may stop for this purpose. We are very desirous of this.

"These are the only objects for which I have sent Commodore Perry, with a powerful squadron, to pay a visit to your imperial majesty's renowned city of Yedo [Tokyo]: friendship, commerce, a supply of coal and provisions, and protection for our ship-wrecked people.

"We have directed Commodore Perry to beg your imperial majesty's acceptance of a few presents. They are of no great value in themselves; but some of them may serve as specimens of the articles manufactured in the United States, and they are intended as tokens of our sincere and respectful friendship.

"May the Almighty have your imperial majesty in His great and holy keeping!"

The letter ended with "Your good friend, Millard Fillmore."

A long silence followed the delivery of the letter. Kayama walked over to the "Prince of Iwami," dropped to his knees and touched the floor with his head as a mark of deep respect. From the "Prince" he received a roll of paper which he carried across the room to Perry.

Again kneeling, he handed the scroll to the Commodore. It was nothing but an official receipt saying that the President's letter had been accepted at Kurihama, "in opposition to Japanese laws," since the Commodore "would feel himself insulted by a refusal to receive the letter at this place." It reminded the Commodore that "this is not a place to negotiate with foreigners."

At such a place there could be no conferences or entertainments.

"Therefore," the Japanese document ended, "as the letter has been received, you can depart."

Perry felt as if he had been slapped on the wrist by a Japanese fan. He did not like the sound of those words "You can depart." He was not used to getting such orders, even from a representative of a high-and-mighty emperor.

The rest of the interview was courteous but cold. Perry made it clear to the Japanese that he did not expect an immediate answer from the Emperor. He said the squadron would leave in two or three days and return in the spring, perhaps in April or May.

By then, he hoped, the Japanese would be ready to answer Fillmore's requests. And then, maybe, the Emperor would be willing to accept the "few presents" from the American President.

"Will the Admiral return with all four ships?" Kayama asked anxiously.

"All of them," Perry's interpreter replied, "and probably more, as these are only a portion of the squadron."

With this repeated threat, the Commodore bowed, turned toward the door and strode out into the brilliant sunshine.

9. Perry Sails Away

As the Commodore marched to the waiting boats, one of the bands struck up "Yankee Doodle" with a gay and impudent air. The tension had eased since Perry and his men had landed to deliver the President's letter.

When Japanese soldiers and civilians pressed in upon them, the Americans stared back at them with indifference, sensing that they were curious rather than hostile. Marines tossed off wisecracks, such as "Jack, give us a chaw of tobacco!"

The sons of Japan looked blank, not understanding a word.

Some of the sailors were bold enough to wander over the beach picking up shells and pebbles as souvenirs. Will Rutherford, the assistant engineer of the *Mississippi*, remembered that his sweetheart in Philadelphia had asked him for a bouquet of Japanese flowers. Back on shipboard, he wrote her:

"All I can send you from Japan is a small pebble stone that I picked up on the beach as we were leaving."

But he gave her a glowing account of the ceremony:

"Oh, my, what a beautiful sight it was! I should have liked my parents and you, my dear, to have seen us landing."

The Americans felt friendly enough to invite Kayama, the so-called Governor, with his chief assistant and two interpreters, to ride the two miles back to Uraga aboard Perry's flagship. This was the first time the Japanese had ever traveled on a steamship.

The guests clambered down into the engine room. There came a torrent of questions, such as "Who invented steamships?" "How fast can they go?"

The Americans showed them pictures of ocean and

river ships, some of them bigger than the *Susque-hanna,* and engravings of New York, New Orleans and San Francisco. When the Japanese turned their curiosity to the officers' revolvers, Captain Buchanan led them to the quarter-deck and fired all six barrels of his revolver in the air.

The Japanese reacted like children seeing the workings of a new toy.

But the Commodore, in his cabin, brooded over three words with which the Japanese had ended the morning ceremony: "You can depart!" Perry's pride was outraged.

No Japanese was going to tell him, in effect, "Get out!" He decided to do the exact opposite.

Without interrupting the shipboard tour of the Japanese visitors, Perry sent for his aide. "We are going up the bay toward Tokyo," he snapped. "We shall send the visitors ashore at Uraga and keep going." The orders were flagged to all other ships of the squadron.

Perry took good care to tell the departing Japanese, through his aide, that he was going up the bay in search of a safer anchorage. The Japanese were shown into their boats. Then the squadron started off around the headland and into the jealously guarded waters of the inner bay.

This time the ships penetrated about ten miles closer to Tokyo. Perry, as usual, sent off surveying groups to test the depth of the water and to see what they could of the forts, the villages and the people on the green and lovely shore.

The Japanese response was not slow in coming. Hardly had the surveying boats begun their job when a boat bearing Kayama caught up with the flagship. The Governor, usually so good-natured, seemed upset.

"Your ships must not go any farther," he said sternly when he had climbed aboard. "If your surveying boats go any closer to land, there will be trouble. The people are already excited at seeing foreigners come so near."

The Americans told him not to worry; the Commodore and his men had come as friends. "Besides," said Perry's interpreter, "if you Japanese came to the United States, you would find our bays and rivers open to you. We wouldn't even keep you from the gold fields of California."

Kayama saw that it would do no good to argue.

One American surveying boat rowed up an inlet into a little river. This was the Americans' first look at the countryside. They were enchanted with what they saw: picturesque villages, and farms so neatly tended that they looked like gardens.

Farmers were working in the rice fields in conical straw hats that shielded them from the summer sun. The hillsides were terraced so that every possible inch could be cultivated for food. Villagers came to the water's edge offering peaches, bigger than those of

Georgia, and pails of water. The Americans showed their friendliness by firing revolvers into the air to amuse the Japanese.

But whenever a good-natured crowd collected on shore, a stern-faced Japanese official appeared and shooed them away. The laws of Japan forbade the people to talk to foreigners, even at a distance.

When Perry heard of the villagers' friendliness, he decided that he, too, would travel up the bay for a closer look at Japan. A traveler's curiosity was not his only reason. The Japanese ruler, he thought, might be more willing to sign a treaty with him on his next visit if the American "Admiral" showed himself at close range in one of his powerful ships.

So the next day Perry transferred his Commodore's pennant to the *Mississippi,* a slightly smaller ship which could float in shallower water. Ten miles from the capital the water was too shallow, and Perry ordered the ship turned back. But even from this distance the Americans could see the low wooden houses of the city's suburbs. Then, as now, Tokyo was one of the biggest cities in the world.

The Japanese did not try to stop Perry's daring foray up the bay. They seemed, in fact, to become friendlier. When Perry returned to his flagship, the Japanese Governor hurried aboard with presents. They included bright silks, interwoven with designs of gold and silver thread, polished lacquer cups and fans decorated with pictures of dragons and devils.

In return Perry presented the Japanese with maps, engravings, pistols and swords. The Governor protested that it was against Japanese law to accept them, but the Americans persuaded him. He took away what he could hide in his baggy robes.

Later the Governor returned bringing chickens and long-tailed Japanese roosters in wicker cages, and several thousand fresh eggs in wooden cases. These delighted the American crewmen, who were bored with salt pork and hard biscuits.

This time the Governor and his companions were jolly and gay. They drank champagne with the American officers. They made flowery speeches of friendship and pretended that they would shed bitter tears when they saw the American ships leave Japan. As good-bye presents the Americans gave them cases of wine and American vegetable seeds to be tried in Japanese fields.

The Governor could not wait to sample the wine until he got ashore. As he sat in his small boat, being rowed back to land, he picked up one of the bottles, knocked off the neck against the side of the boat and drank to the Americans' good health and good luck.

On July 17, 1853, Perry's black ships were ready to leave. Again the steamers towed the two sailing sloops out toward the ocean. Hundreds of Japanese lined the shore to watch them depart.

The wind freshened as the squadron lost sight of

Mount Fuji and the green shores of Japan. Soon the ships were wallowing in a fierce Pacific typhoon.

On deck everything movable had been lashed down. Below deck, where the crewmen slept, shoes and sea chests sloshed around in salt water that poured down the hatchways. The waves were mountainous. The four ships lost sight of one another as they dipped deep into the troughs and pitched high up onto the crests. The seas swept across the bows and sterns with such fury that one of Commodore Perry's own boats was washed away.

The Commodore, who had lived through worse storms than this, was not worried. As he looked back upon his first visit to Japan, he was well satisfied.

But he wondered what was going on inside Japan. Were the Japanese plotting delays and obstructions to American demands? Would they resist with force when he returned, as he had promised, in the spring?

10. A Look Behind the Screens

If Perry had known what was happening inside Japan, he might have knocked even more boldly at the door of the forbidden empire.

The Japanese were terrified when the Commodore's squadron first appeared. Thousands in Tokyo, the capital, were on the edge of panic at the news that great black ships had anchored in the bay. The size and the death-dealing power of these ships grew more frightening with every rumor and story.

For the first few days after Perry's arrival, the Tokyo streets were choked with men, women and children carrying household belongings on their backs or on small hand carts. Everyone, it seemed, wanted to escape from the city to places of safety in the country. The people believed that Perry's guns could blow them and their little wooden houses to smithereens.

The Japanese government, too, was panicky, and for an understandable reason. Tokyo in those days had almost two million people. Since roads in Japan were poor and the means of transportation were slow and primitive, most of the rice for feeding Tokyo had to come from the farms by sea.

It came in barges that crept along the coasts from north and south into Tokyo Bay. Perry's guns could easily have sunk the barges or set them on fire. He could have starved Tokyo by cutting off its rice supply.

Of all this, and more, Perry was not aware. He knew that Japan had woven a cocoon around itself for more than two hundred years. He did not know, and could not have known, that the Japanese were living through a hard and bitter time.

The people were hungry and discontented. Taxes were so high, and varied so much from year to year, that tens of thousands of farmers poured into the cities in the hope of earning a better living.

Shut off from the outer world, strictly forbidden to trade or travel abroad, the Japanese had lived in unbroken peace. But it was the peace-and-quiet of a stifling room in which doors and windows were tightly locked.

Japanese artists developed their own special style of painting their native birds, their blossoming trees and flowers, and the peak of Mount Fuji. In many ways their decorated screens and scrolls were more delicate, more poetic than the paintings of western Europe. But by the time Perry arrived, even this superb art was growing stale for lack of new ideas.

Life inside a cocoon had another bad result for Japan. It kept the people ignorant of the outer world and therefore afraid of it. Because Japan was afraid, it thought of all Westerners as "barbarians." In their weakness the Japanese comforted themselves with the thought that they were somehow more civilized than anyone else.

Big noses, bulging eyes, hairy chests—these disgusted the Japanese whenever they saw the Dutch traders who, alone among Westerners, had been allowed to keep a trading post in Nagasaki harbor. The Japanese contrasted these features with their own small noses, their almond eyes and smoother skins, and they assumed that of course they were better than these uncouth Westerners. They felt the same contempt for Europeans that the ancient Romans felt for the brawnier, hairier barbarians of the northern forests.

But there was one small hole in the wall that surrounded Japan. This was the Dutch trading station. Japanese scholars peeped through the hole and caught a tiny glimpse of the great world outside. A few Dutch books and Western ideas trickled through the hole into Japan—not many, but enough to prove to educated Japanese that their country was being left behind in a swiftly changing world.

From Dutch books, students found out about Western science, the growth of armies and navies in Europe, the spread of European empires, the rise of the United States.

From Nakahama Manjiro, a young Japanese castaway who had spent several years in America, they learned something about the young Republic across the Pacific—about George Washington, the Mexican War, the coming of the railroads, the gold rush to California. This explains why the Japanese officials asked intelligent questions about America when they boarded Perry's flagship in Tokyo Bay.

"The people of America are upright and generous, and do no evil," Nakahama wrote. "Among them there are neither murders nor robberies, as a rule. If such things occur, there are laws covering them, and the offenders are promptly seized.

"For their wedding ceremony, the Americans merely make a proclamation to the gods and become married, after which they usually go on a sightseeing trip to the mountains.

"Husband and wife are exceedingly affectionate to each other, and the happiness of the home is unparalleled in other countries. The women do not use rouge, powder and the like."

Whether or not they believed every word of this, many educated Japanese felt it was time to get rid of the closed-door policy. They risked arrest in reading foreign books, for the government's spies were everywhere. A few brave scholars took the risk. Secretly they resolved that Japan must catch up with other countries.

Perry knew, from his reading, that there were two rulers of Japan. One was the man who held the title of emperor, or Mikado. He was a shadowy and holy personage who lived at Kyoto in a palace surrounded by a huge wall. None of his people ever saw him except for the few noblemen who served him.

The second ruler, the man who held the political power, was the Shogun. He lived in a palace behind a watery moat in the middle of Tokyo. The Shogun belonged to a family of military dictators, the Tokugawas, who had seized power at the end of the sixteenth century. It was one of the first Tokugawa Shoguns who had expelled foreigners, slaughtered Christians and shut Japan off from the outer world.

The Shogun even sent spies to watch the Emperor in Kyoto!

But Perry did not know that the Shogun of 1853 was weak, or that many powerful Japanese families were plotting against him. When Perry's black ships arrived, the Shogun's councilors were uncertain whether they could count on the loyalty of the great landowners, who used to obey the slightest orders from the palace.

The Shogun's government was too unsure of itself to accept or reject the Americans' demands. Therefore, delay was decided upon, and a decree was issued saying:

"Our policy shall be to evade any definite answer to the Americans' request for the opening of ports, while at the same time maintaining a peaceful demeanor.

"It may be, however, that they will have recourse to violence. For that, we must be prepared, lest the country suffer disgrace. Therefore every possible effort will be made to prepare means of defense. Above all, everyone must practice patience, refrain from anger, and carefully observe the conduct of the foreigners.

"Should they open hostilities, all must at once take up arms and fight strenuously for the country."

Half-heartedly, as if knowing it was useless, local governors along the coast began to drill soldiers and build stone walls around the miserable forts which Perry had seen from his first anchorage.

In the midst of this last-minute effort, the Shogun

died in his Tokyo castle. His death gave his advisers a happy idea.

Couldn't they use the event as an excuse to put off Perry's second arrival in Japan? Delay was their only weapon. They asked the Dutch to transmit a message to the Commodore, who was then resting his men and refitting his ships at Hong Kong, off the southern coast of China.

The message said the Shogun had died; there would have to be a long period of mourning, and in the confusion there would be no government to deal with.

The word "confusion" was the literal truth. For weeks the great families of Japan plotted and intrigued until they finally agreed on a successor to the dead ruler. They forgot all about Perry, as if his visit had been nothing but a bad dream.

Suddenly, on a freezing February morning in 1854, guards outside the Shogun's castle heard the clop-clopping of horsemen galloping toward the gates. Soon the horsemen were inside the castle, falling to their knees before the new Shogun, a muddle-headed young man who had just taken power. They had serious and unwelcome news.

The American barbarians were back!

"It cannot be true," the Shogun said. "They said they would come in the spring. This is only February."

The kneeling messengers touched their foreheads to the floor, as if begging for mercy.

"It is true. We saw the ships ourselves."

"Where are they heading?"

"They were steering straight for Tokyo Bay, where they anchored last summer."

The Shogun whipped out his fan and held it in front of his face, perhaps to hide his anger. Then he asked:

"How many ships did you see?"

"One sailing ship is already anchored in the bay. Two others are approaching Kamakura, near the entrance, and three black ships, with steam, are following them."

Still on their knees, still trembling and lowering their heads again and again, the messengers half crawled out of the audience chamber.

11. Back With More Guns

The black ships were back in Japanese waters at least
two months earlier than the Shogun's unhappy government had expected them.

There were more of them now, more than the Japanese had ever seen in a foreign fleet. Perry had made
good his parting threat that he would return with "a
larger force" in the spring.

The squadron he now commanded was the most powerful that the United States had ever sent on a foreign mission. It numbered three steam warships, five other warships under sail and two supply ships carrying food and other stores for an eight months' stay in Japan.

The fleet had thirty-eight eight-inch guns, four nine-inch guns and a bristling array of smaller cannon. The guns were enough to demolish the paper-thin forts of the Japanese, and to spread havoc in the coastal cities if they ever had to be fired.

Two thousand sailors and marines, trained for battle or any other emergency, manned the squadron.

The Commodore meant business. He would follow his instructions not to use force unless attacked. But he would not let the Japanese deceive him, delay him or block his announced purpose of opening Japan to American ships and trade.

A streak of suspicion in the old sailor's character warned him that the Japanese were probably trying to hoodwink him. Behind their masks of politeness, weren't they playing a cat-and-mouse game to avoid answering the President's letter? It seemed to Perry that they had seized upon the death of the Shogun as a convenient excuse to block his return. He thought these tactics had a fishy smell about them, and he was not going to allow Japanese mourning or anything else to delay his mission.

There was another reason why Perry wanted an agreement as quickly as possible. While he was in Hong Kong, between voyages, he heard that four Russian warships had visited the Japanese port of Nagasaki. They had left a letter from their government, had held meetings with Japanese officials and had then sailed off to China.

Perry also noticed that a French warship, anchored near Hong Kong, had sailed away suddenly under secret orders. If Russia and France intended to deal with Japan and win privileges for their ships, Perry was determined to forestall them.

He ordered four sailing ships to set out for Japan ahead of the steamers, since they would take longer to get there. Then, on February 7, 1854, he left Okinawa, an island 900 miles southwest of Tokyo, with three powerful steam frigates: the *Susquehanna,* the *Mississippi* and the *Powhatan.* The first two, of course, had been with him on his first visit to Japan. The *Powhatan,* one of the newest and most heavily armed ships of the Navy, had joined him to reinforce the squadron on its second voyage.

A wintry storm did its best to give Perry a bone-chilling welcome as he approached Japan for the second time. In the previous summer the sea and sky had been blue and friendly. This time the squadron butted slowly up the Japanese coast against an icy wind and heavy seas. Spray froze on the decks; officers and men shivered and held their ears to keep warm.

The shores of Japan, so green in the summertime, looked gray and somber. Mount Fuji was a cone of purest white, covered with snow from base to summit.

As the steamers churned toward the entrance of Tokyo Bay, their watch officers saw two American ships near the shore, apparently at anchor. These were two of Perry's sailing ships sent ahead from China. Soon a signal announced: "*Macedonian* is ashore!" The sailing corvette *Macedonian* had gone aground off Kamakura, the thirteenth-century capital of Japan.

Its companion, the sailing sloop *Vandalia*, was anchored near by, unable to help. Perry ordered the *Mississippi*, with her steam engines, to pull the stricken ship off the rocks.

When the *Macedonian* had been refloated, the three steamers, each with a sailing ship in tow, moved proudly up the bay. They stopped at the same place where Perry had anchored the year before. There they found the *Southampton*, which had reached the shelter of the bay the day before and had escaped the worst of the storm.

Again the Japanese officials rushed out in little boats to meet them. If they were surprised by Perry's unexpectedly early arrival, they were too polite to show it. They bowed and introduced themselves.

Kayama, the "Governor," whom the Americans had come to know and like, was not among them. He was reported ill, and did not reappear for several days. The welcomers this time included three gray-robed strangers who peered at the Americans with gimlet eyes.

The Japanese described them as "the cross-eyed persons," or men who look in all directions. It was a true description, for they were clearly official spies.

Now the Japanese and the Americans began a ten-day battle of wits. The subject was where to hold a conference at which the Japanese would present their answer to President Fillmore's letter. They wanted Perry to come to Uraga for this meeting, or to Kamakura, where the *Macedonian* had gone aground, or to the old landing place at Kurihama. The Commodore was secretly determined that the meeting place should be within gun range of a safe anchorage, and as near Tokyo as possible.

Day after day, on the Commodore's orders, the Americans stood firm. To the horror of the Japanese, the Americans threatened to take the squadron all the way up to Tokyo and hold the conference there. To show that this was not an idle threat, Perry finally ordered his squadron eight miles up the bay nearer the capital.

This broke the deadlock. The Japanese agreed that the talks should be held at the little village of Yokohama, now Japan's greatest seaport, only fifteen miles from the Shogun's palace. Perry promptly lined up his ships opposite Yokohama and ordered them to anchor with their guns commanding the shore.

The array of black ships and bristling guns caused a sensation in the crowded cities near their new anchorage. Morning and evening the ships' bands played. On one warm day seventy thousand people crowded the beach and the surrounding hillsides where they could hear the music, the ships' bells and the sentry calls.

This time the Japanese were more hospitable, offering coal, water, wood—anything the American visitors might need. They brought vegetables, oranges, chickens and eggs to the flagship. For the Commodore's special pleasure they included sweet cakes and oysters. Perry's officers could hardly believe their ears when Kayama announced:

"My Government knows you Americans better than it did last year. It has entire confidence in the Americans now. Therefore, there will be no Japanese soldiers when the Commodore comes ashore at Yokohama."

Such friendliness seemed—and was—too good to be true. Underneath the surface of good fellowship, the Americans sensed that this was no game they were playing. It was more like a fencing match near the edge of a precipice. And at times they came perilously close to the edge. They were always on the alert for treachery.

Once, while Captain Adams was conferring on the shore, through an interpreter, with a group of Japanese, he heard what sounded like the crack of a rifle. All the Americans in the small landing party clapped their hands to their pistols. For a moment they froze,

The officer lunged forward and saved the sailor

fingers on the triggers, ready to trade bullet for bullet.

What they heard was not a pistol shot at all. One of the Japanese officials, probably as a practical joke, had snapped his fan shut with a sharp crack. With perfect unconcern he put on his eyeglasses and began solemnly to study the calling cards of the American officers. If the whole thing was a trick, the Japanese did not betray the fact by so much as a flicker of an eyelid.

On another occasion a Japanese with two swords, one long and one short, managed to get into one of the rowboats that was carrying officials out to Perry's flagship. He planned to kill the Commodore and then to stab himself. As he reached the boarding ladder, he caught sight of an officer whom he took to be Perry at the rail. Stealthily he unsheathed one of his swords.

At that moment a sailor on the flagship lost his balance, and would have fallen overboard if the officer had not lunged forward and saved him. The assassin quietly put his sword back and mingled with the rest of the Japanese group on board.

He explained his change of heart later by saying that a "great lord" who would save the life of a humble sailor was not a man whom Japan needed to fear.

Perry probably never heard this story, which was not published until more than fifty years later. But it showed what dark forces were stirring under the smooth surface of Japanese life. Perry did well to be on his guard as the treaty-making discussions began.

12. A Show of Power

The Japanese had told Perry that they would not bring
soldiers to the treaty-making conference at Yokohama.
Secretly they broke their promise.

They hid hundreds of armed men behind the hand-
some building they had put up for the meeting. The
harbor swarmed with small boats gaily decorated as
if to welcome Perry. But their crews were armed and

under orders to fight to the death if the Americans fired a shot.

The Americans, too, had made a promise. Perry's officers had agreed to bring only a "guard of honor" with the Commodore. In pledging this, they were no more sincere than were the Japanese. They did not say how big the ceremonial guard would be.

In truth the Americans came ashore more like an invading army than a friendly "guard of honor." Twenty-seven boats, crammed with 500 armed men, converged on the beach. In the background, forming a barrier across the harbor, Perry's black ships trained their guns on the crowded shoreline.

The marines and sailors jumped out and lined up, shoulder to shoulder, in two two-deep rows of men at right angles to the water's edge. Between the two rows a corridor about two hundred yards wide was left open for Perry's procession.

The Commodore's salute crashed from the *Macedonian*. The combined ships' bands began an oompah-oompah as a kind of overture. As Perry stepped ashore, in full-dress uniform with sword and cocked hat, the marines presented arms with a clash of weapons that could be heard far away.

The bands swung into "Hail, Columbia!" and the Commodore, acting even more pompous than usual, strutted slowly up the beach to the conference hall.

At first the Japanese had stretched canvas screens all the way from the water to the building, so that the townspeople would not be able to see the procession. But Perry's officers sent word that the Commodore would not think of landing until the screens were taken down.

As a result the Commodore had a densely packed audience of Japanese men, women and children peeping from behind the marines as he paraded by.

The Japanese saw that the black-and-white striped flag of their Shogun was fluttering from the masthead of the American flagship. It was the first time the Shogun's emblem had flown from a foreign warship in more than two hundred years.

As another American gesture of respect, a twenty-one-gun salute was fired for the Emperor and another of seventeen guns in honor of Hayashi, the chief of the five Japanese commissioners appointed to deal with Perry. Hayashi was an eminent and respected figure in Japan. He was not a politician, but a leading scholar, the Lord Rector of the University of Tokyo.

Since Perry's first visit this man had used his influence with the Shogun in favor of peace with the Americans. Perry felt he had scored a real triumph when Hayashi was chosen to head the Japanese delegation. Now, for the first time, the Commodore was to bargain with a man of his own stature, a man who really spoke for the Shogun.

Hayashi and the four other commissioners bowed gravely as Perry entered the dimly lighted hall. Lesser officials were crouching on their knees in front of the dignitaries. One of them, still on his knees, pushed himself with his arms across the floor to where Perry's translator was standing. He had a message for the Commodore.

"The Prince is glad to see you, and hopes your health is better," the message said. The Japanese always called Hayashi a "prince," although he really was just a professor. Perry sent a similar greeting, and the courier, still on his knees, seemed to be hopping across the room like a frog.

The Japanese then got down to business. They invited Perry and four of his officers to come into a small back room, behind an enormous purple flag, for a private talk with the five commissioners. At once they produced a roll of paper with an official seal on it. This was the long-awaited answer to President Fillmore's letter which Perry had delivered at Kurihama eight months before.

Behind its polite language the answer spelled one word: delay. "It is quite impossible," the letter said, "to give satisfactory answers all at once to the proposals of your government, as it is most positively forbidden by the laws of our imperial ancestors."

But—and this gave Perry some pleasure—the letter said Japan would provide coal, wood, water and food for American ships, and would take care of ships and crews in distress. Japan would open one harbor, but not for another five years. As for coal and food, the letter asked, how much would Perry need?

The Commodore was not going to argue. He had a hunch that the Japanese had no power to stand up against his ships and guns. He was ready to stay for six months if necessary to wear them down and get what he wanted.

His answer was mild, with a threat behind it. He pulled out of his inner pocket two documents which he asked the Japanese to study. One was a copy of the commercial treaty already signed by the United States and China. The other was a draft of a similar treaty which he hoped the Japanese would sign. "I have been sent here by my government to make a treaty with yours," the Commodore said. "If I do not succeed now, my government will probably send more ships here to make one.

"We did not come here to fight with you. We came on a friendly mission, and our squadron is a very small one. If we had come to make war on you, we would have brought three or four times as many ships."

This, of course, was bluff. The squadron was not a "very small" one; it was the biggest that had ever left the United States. Young Will Rutherford of the *Mississippi*, eavesdropping outside the purple-flagged door, thought Perry's talk was "all a hoax."

"He was trying to frighten the Japanese," Rutherford wrote later, "but they are not so easily bluffed as one would imagine."

The Japanese promised to read Perry's documents,

but, as usual, they did not say when, or how, they would answer.

Toward the end of the three-hour interview, Perry made two new requests. One of them was not too difficult for the Japanese to accept. The Commodore said his men would need exercise after being cooped up on the ships for so long. He would like permission for them to go ashore and walk in the countryside, with the understanding that they would stay within a few miles of Yokohama.

The second request puzzled the Japanese so much that they asked for time to consult privately about it. Leaving Perry in the back room, with Japanese soup, fish, fruit and cake to help him pass the time, the commissioners went outside to consider an odd and upsetting problem.

13. Japan Buries an "Ancient Law"

Robert Williams, one of Perry's marines, had died of a brain illness. The Commodore asked the Japanese commissioners if the United States could buy a piece of ground for burying the dead marine and other Americans who might die on the expedition.

This was only a part of the problem which so perplexed the Japanese officials. The location Perry suggested was on an island in the bay which the Americans had named Webster Island, in honor of Daniel Webster, the former Secretary of State.

Perry had had his eye on this island ever since his first landing. It might be useful someday as a small naval base.

As if the Japanese sensed what was in Perry's mind, they objected strongly to a burial place on the island. Instead they offered a piece of ground alongside a temple on the mainland, a quarter of a mile from the conference hall. There, they said, the marine could have a Christian burial.

This was a big concession. For more than two hundred years it had been a crime, punishable by death, to hold any Christian service on Japanese soil. The Shoguns who outlawed Christianity in the seventeenth century did not object to the religion as such. They feared the Christian missionaries, especially the Spanish and Portuguese, as agents of foreign powers that wanted to conquer Japan.

Even in Perry's day the ban was ironclad, and no Japanese dared to violate it. A few days before the landing at Yokohama, a town official, visiting the *Mississippi,* had been asked to write his name on the title page of a Book of Common Prayer. The page had an engraving of the Cross on it.

The official wet his camel's-hair brush with his lips, dipped it into his portable inkstand and was about to sign his name in Japanese characters. Suddenly his eye fell on the picture of the Cross. He shook his head, threw the book on the table, and no amount of urging could make him touch it again.

In Japan a hundred years ago the Cross produced somewhat the same reaction as the Communist hammer-and-sickle does in America today. Even so, the Japanese were willing to let a Christian burial take place on their soil.

Perry was impressed. He thanked the commissioners and said he would be happy to see them aboard his ship as soon as the cold and windy March weather changed. Past lines of bowing Japanese he left the hall to go back to his squadron. Again the bands played, the drums rolled and the marines presented arms as the Commodore walked stiffly down the beach to his barge.

The chaplain, the Reverend George Jones, hurried to Perry's cabin to ask for instructions.

"I am not sure, sir, how far they will let me go in a funeral service," he said.

"Do exactly as you always do on such occasions—no more, no less," Perry answered.

"But how should I act if they interrupt me?"

"Still go on and have your usual service," the Commodore said.

The chaplain, deeply troubled, said he would try to follow Perry's advice. He had read that over the tombs of thousands of massacred Christians, one of the old Shoguns had long ago put this inscription:

"So long as the sun shall warm the earth, let no Christian be so bold as to come to Japan; and let all know that the King of Spain himself, or the Christian's God, or the great God of all, if he violates this command, shall pay for it with his head."

The next day a slow-moving funeral parade wound through the streets of Yokohama. Instead of turning their backs on it in fear or horror, men, women and children ran to the main street from all parts of the village as they heard the sound of the fifes and muffled drums.

The youngsters of Yokohama raced up the street as soon as the flag-draped coffin had passed, and found new curbstone seats in order to watch the procession all over again. Some pointed with excitement at the marines carrying their rifles upside down, as naval regulations required.

Some pointed at the chaplain, who walked alone, carrying his prayer book. One woman held up her baby to see the foreigner in his unfamiliar white robes.

The procession moved slowly to a wooded hill outside the town, where steps led up to a Buddhist temple through carved wooden gateways. A Buddhist priest led the way to the grave, dug near a field where the ashes of long-dead Japanese had been buried.

The marines and sailors took off their caps. As Chaplain Jones began to recite the prayers for the dead, he could see that the hills near by were covered with at least two thousand people watching quietly and attentively.

The Buddhist priest squatted on a mat near the graveside, reciting the funeral service of his own ancient religion. On a table in front of him he burned incense, blessed a cup of Buddhist holy water and rang a small bell from time to time. Folding his hands inside his robe and bowing his head, he intoned the Buddhist prayers in a low voice.

The body was lowered into the grave. The marines fired three volleys into the air, and the procession moved back into the village. The old priest was still praying when the Americans left.

The funeral, unimportant in itself, was one of the most important events of Perry's visit. The Americans had buried a marine; the Japanese had buried one of their "ancient laws," the forbidding of Christian ceremonies.

Four other men of the expedition died before Perry sailed for home. For each the Japanese provided burial ground and permitted a full Christian funeral service on shore. And each time the Japanese crowds looked on with interest and respect.

14. Sam Patch Has a Fright

In all their dealings with Perry and his men, the Japanese seldom showed surprise at anything. It was part of their code of conduct to conceal their emotions in the presence of strangers. But now they were to have a shock so upsetting that they did not even try to hide their feelings.

On one of Kayama's visits to the squadron, Captain

Adams handed him a letter written in Japanese characters, and asked if he would deliver it when he got ashore.

"Who is this from?" Kayama asked. He saw that the letter was addressed, not to an official or a nobleman, but to ordinary Japanese in Tokyo.

"It is from a Japanese in our crew," Adams answered.

A Japanese in the American Navy! The man must be a traitor. What was his name?

"I do not know his real name," said Adams. "We call him Sam Patch."

Kayama made an effort to control his anger and dismay. "I will deliver the letter," he promised. "But I would like to see this man." Adams assured him that he could.

Although Kayama could hardly believe it, Adams had told the truth. Sam Patch was one of seventeen Japanese seamen whose boat had been swept far from the shores of Japan in 1851 by a typhoon. An American merchant ship had rescued them and taken them to San Francisco. There they were kept for a whole year aboard an American revenue cutter.

An American warship, the *St. Mary's,* took them to China and transferred them to the bigger warship, the *Susquehanna,* which was stationed in Shanghai as part of the Navy's China squadron.

American officers treated the seventeen men as

lower than the lowliest seamen, and forced them to do the hardest and most menial tasks.

When the castaways heard that the *Susquehanna* had joined Perry's squadron and would sail soon for Japan, sixteen of them left the ship and were swallowed up in the teeming crowds of Shanghai. They knew that any Japanese citizen who violated the law by going abroad was in danger of death when he got home. It would be better, they thought, to take their chances in China than to have their heads chopped off by an executioner of the Shogun.

Only Sam Patch preferred to stay aboard. Some streak of adventure in him, some faith in these overbearing Americans, made him willing to risk a return to his homeland.

On the *Susquehanna* he became a member of the crew. He put on an American seaman's uniform and began to feel like a free man. He tried to look like an American and behaved like one. Instead of shaving the sides of his head and tying the remaining hair into a Japanese topknot, he let his hair grow all over his head, as Americans did.

But all the way from Shanghai to the Japanese coast, and while the ships were anchored in forbidden Japanese waters, the Americans made poor Sam Patch the butt of jokes. They regarded him as a comic character because of his few words of twisted English and his deeply ingrained habit of bowing to superiors. They teased him without mercy.

"Sam, it will be too bad for you when we get to Japan!"

"Sam, be careful of that head of yours; they'll chop it off!"

Sometimes a smirking gesture, of a hand passed across his throat, suggested better than words the fate that awaited him.

Sam had enough spirit to stand the teasing. When the *Susquehanna* anchored off Yokohama, he persuaded a junior officer to ask the Japanese officials to forward a letter to his friends in Tokyo. This was the letter that was handed to the astonished Kayama.

A few days later Sam Patch was summoned aft to the Captain's cabin to meet the Governor. He wore a clean American uniform. His newly grown hair was combed in American fashion.

But when he caught his first sight of the Japanese dignitary in his silken robes, his face turned a ghastly green, as if he were seasick. Completely awe-stricken, he crouched down on his knees, his face to the deck, his whole body trembling with terror.

Poor Sam thought his last hour had come.

"Get up, Sam," said Captain Adams, half sternly, half reassuringly. "You are on an American warship now. You are perfectly safe—as safe as any one of the crew. There's nothing to be afraid of."

Sam could not be comforted. The sight of his countrymen with their swords, the fear of being beheaded, was too much for him. In a few terrifying moments he seemed to have lost all the confidence he had gained as a member of an American crew. Somehow he was back in the many-layered society of Japan, in which a humble man groveled in the dust in the presence of a superior.

Kayama said nothing during this encounter, but he did not fail to report the meeting to his government. Later the Japanese made an official request to Commodore Perry to send Sam Patch ashore. This time the Commodore himself became Sam's protector. He gave these instructions to his officers, who were to deal personally with the Japanese:

"I have no objection whatever to this man staying in Japan if he wants to stay. But it must be by his own free will. And the Japanese must give a written pledge that the man will not in any way be punished for his absence from Japan.

"Remember that he was shipwrecked. He was thrown by God's providence on American protection. He came aboard an American warship by his own choice. For all these reasons, he is entitled to the protection and security of an American citizen. Therefore I can allow no force to be used to make him stay in Japan after we leave."

When this firm message was relayed to the Japanese officials, they ridiculed the idea that Sam would be punished in any way.

"We will gladly give any guarantee you want," they said. "He will not be molested. We will return him at once to his friends. They are very anxious to see him."

Sam was called to the Captain's cabin. Again he turned pale and shivered, and fell to his knees as he saw the Japanese officials. Lieutenant Silas Bent, one of Perry's aides, ordered him sharply to stand up. Bent was disgusted that anyone could be so servile, so cringing, on the deck of an American warship and under the American flag.

Sam listened to the Japanese as they pleaded with him to come back. He turned his eyes away from theirs and trembled. Nothing could coax him to leave the ship.

By now the sailors who had teased Sam on the way to Japan had begun to like him and feel sorry for him. After all, he was a good-natured fellow; he was trying to do his job as a member of the American crew.

One of the marines named Goble took a special interest in him and began teaching him English and Christianity. Sam's English improved, although, like most Japanese, he never could pronounce the letter "l" and always, for example, said "forrow" rather than "follow." In the end Goble took Sam as a companion and friend to his own farm in upstate New York.

But for the remainder of Perry's stay in Japanese waters Sam Patch was so fearful that he refused to get into a boat for trips to the shore. Whenever his countrymen came aboard the ship, he kept out of sight.

The Japanese pried around the ship without ever seeing him. They even peered into the hold in search of Sam.

What they saw aroused their curiosity and almost made them forget the missing sailor. The hold was piled high with oddly shaped boxes and bundles ready for unloading. The visitors longed to know what was inside, but were too polite to ask.

The Americans pretended not to notice their curiosity. It amused them to think that the contents of these parcels were going to surprise the Japanese even more than had the sight of Sam Patch.

15. Magic Gifts From Perry

When Perry planned his expedition to Japan, he spent much time, thought, and government money in finding and choosing gifts to take along. He knew that in the Orient the exchange of gifts was a part of good manners.

You never visited anyone without bringing presents to show your friendliness; and your host responded with presents for you. When you represented your government on a mission to another government, your gifts had to be lavish. They were supposed to show the power, the riches and the glory of your country.

Perry was determined to impress the Japanese with the presents he would bring. But his ideas were out of the ordinary. He made up his mind not only to flatter the Japanese but also to surprise them. His gifts would be like nothing the Japanese emperors had ever received in the earlier centuries, when Japan entertained high-ranking visitors from the royal courts of Asia.

The Commodore had some presents specially made, bought many others and wangled still others from manufacturers, free of charge. When the treaty negotiations began to show some prospect of success, he decided that the time had come to present the gifts to the Japanese commissioners. He hoped to help the treaty discussions along by letting them see the presents he had brought for their Emperor.

The showman in Perry decided to make the presentation more than a ceremony. It would be a party, with fun and games, mystery and suspense—an occasion the Japanese would long remember.

On a wet and windy morning of March, 1854, launches, heavily laden with bales and packages, splashed through the whitecaps from Perry's ships to the shore. A company of marines and one of the ships' bands went along to draw attention to the arrival of the presents.

Captain Abbot of the *Macedonian,* who was in charge of the landing, found Hayashi inside the treaty house and presented a formal letter from Perry delivering the gifts.

On the level ground above the beach there was a din of hammering and unpacking of crates. American seamen did most of the work, but the Japanese went to great lengths to be helpful. They even built sheds where the presents would be safe from the rain.

Perry saw to it that the first presents to be opened were the least impressive. Nevertheless, the Japanese grinned with joy at seeing big boxes of rifles, muskets, swords and pistols, almost a hundred weapons in all. Now they could have the fun of shooting off firearms instead of watching the Americans do it!

Next came endless barrels and cases of whisky, wine and liqueurs. A few of the Japanese had sampled these on their visits to the American ships—with hilarious results.

Less conventional presents were a telescope for the Emperor and a number of clocks. The Americans did not realize until they landed that the Japanese knew how to make clocks, an art they had learned from Portuguese traders in the sixteenth century. A box of perfumes had been included for the Empress, in case there was such a lady in Japan. The Japanese interpreters fell eagerly on a box of big books. One was Webster's Dictionary, invaluable for Japanese who wanted to learn English.

As if to prove that Americans were not uncultured "barbarians," Perry had chosen Audubon's magnificently illustrated *Birds of America* and his three volumes on American Quadrupeds. Audubon was one of the glories of the young United States.

The Commodore rightly guessed that his graceful, vibrant pictures of birds, beasts and flowers would appeal strongly to the Japanese, who had excelled for centuries in painting birds and flowers.

But Perry was not chiefly interested in culture. He wanted to boast about American inventive skill and scientific genius. He chose examples designed to impress the Japanese and also to be useful to them.

Out of the bales and boxes came almost two hundred farm tools in common use in the United States. They ranged in size all the way from wagons and carts to shovels, hoes, trowels and shears for clipping sheep. The man in charge of them was Dr. James Morrow, a South Carolinian whom Perry had taken along as official agriculturist with his expedition.

Morrow's bag of tricks included two grindstones, the first the Japanese had ever seen. Imagine sharpening knives on wheels of stone whirled by pedals! While Japanese civilians as well as officials crowded around him, he produced extension ladders, something like the

Best of all the presents was a shiny black locomotive

ladders used by firemen today in fighting a blaze in a high building.

Morrow delighted the Japanese by showing how a suction hose pumped water from a well and then sprayed it on a housetop. At one time he had an audience of more than two hundred. Stately officials amused themselves by wetting house roofs and throwing water over them into the treetops. The crowd scattered in all directions "with a great laugh," Morrow wrote in his diary, when the hose was suddenly turned on them.

Perry's greatest surprises were still to come. The Americans stretched a wire along the beach for a mile between the treaty house and what they called a "receiving station." At either end they attached batteries, insulators and other strange-looking gadgets. Then they began clack-clacking the first telegraph messages ever heard in Japan.

The Japanese would not believe that messages could travel faster than the wind. They decided to outrace the telegraph to see whether these Americans were playing a trick on them. It was no use. Each time they sprinted the mile from the treaty house to the receiving station, the message had arrived ahead of them!

The telegraph caused a sensation. The Japanese resolved that they, too, would learn how to flash words in this magic way.

Best of all the presents was the biggest of all—a shiny black locomotive, with a tender and passenger car. Perry had ordered a scale model exactly one-fourth the size of railroad engines and cars in the United States. Gangs of seamen unloaded 370 feet of circular track, one-fourth the usual width. The tracks laid, the little engine and its cars were placed on the rail. A wood fire crackled in the boiler.

The whistle tooted, smoke and steam poured out of the five-foot smokestack and the train chugged gaily around the track, to the shouts and shrieks of the Japanese who crowded around.

The little train picked up speed until it was spanking along at eighteen miles an hour. Then it stopped, and the Americans offered to give Japanese officials their first railroad ride.

One of the treaty commissioners, usually dignified and solemn, could not resist the temptation. Since the passenger car was too tiny to hold anyone bigger than a baby, the commissioner climbed on top of it and held tight. His robes billowed in the wind as the train whirled him around the circle. The representative of the Shogun giggled like a little boy on a merry-go-round.

For weeks afterward the model railway held the Japanese spellbound. Thousands walked the fifteen miles from Tokyo to see it. One was a learned man who brought with him a Dutch book on the steam engine. He compared the pictures in his book with the parts of the miniature steam engine—hoping, no doubt, to build a similar locomotive in Japan.

Nobody, it seemed, was too high-and-mighty to want to see this marvel that Perry had brought for the Emperor.

One day a high nobleman came by barge to inspect the railway. When he walked up the beach, hundreds of Japanese recognized him and fell to their knees. They touched their heads to the ground as a sign of absolute submission and respect.

Dr. Morrow, the farm expert, was on the beach at the time.

"Who is he?" Morrow whispered to one of the Japanese interpreters. The Japanese was silent until the exalted stranger had passed. Then he said:

"I think it is the Shogun himself—in disguise."

Perhaps even the ruler of Japan could not resist the charm of a model railroad.

16. Wrestlers Grunt and Heave

The Japanese, of course, were not going to let Perry outdo them in generosity. Eleven days after the American gift party, they invited the Commodore ashore to receive Japanese presents in return.

At first Perry and his officers were dazzled. They found the treaty hall piled high with rich brocades, lacquered tables, writing desks and polished goblets.

The Commodore particularly admired some porcelain of wonderful lightness and transparency, decorated with birds and flowers in gold.

These were the things which educated Japanese prized in Perry's day. The Americans had brought alcoholic liquor; the Japanese responded with flowered writing paper and vases. The Americans had given firearms; the Japanese, a lacquered bookcase. Hayashi's gifts included 400 specimens of Japanese sea shells. The shells hardly appealed to American naval officers, but the Lord Rector of the University knew that the United States had scholars and naturalists who might find them priceless.

As the Americans looked more closely at the silk and lacquer ware, they decided that the Japanese gifts were far less valuable than their own. The Commodore himself thought it was a shabby display. Perhaps the Japanese had not given of their best because they secretly looked down on the Americans, as on all Westerners, as "barbarians." Edward McCauley of the *Powhatan* whispered, "There's nothing here that couldn't be made better in the United States!"

As if sensing Perry's disappointment, the Japanese invited him into a small adjoining room to receive presents that might be more to the Navy's taste. They gave him three matchlocks (old-fashioned rifles) and two swords, as symbols of Japan's martial spirit.

Finally, in a burst of friendship, they handed the Commodore two complete sets of Japanese coins. This was a violation of Japanese laws; it had long been a crime to give Japanese money to foreigners.

If Perry thought he could gather up his staggering load of presents and make a dignified retreat to his flagship, he was mistaken. The day was young. The Japanese had several more surprises in store for him.

The first was a mountain of rice—200 bags of it, each bag weighing 140 pounds. The bags were stacked on the beach, ready to be loaded into Perry's boats.

"Why rice?" was the question in the Americans' minds. They would have preferred a little fresh meat to vary the salt pork and hardtack of shipboard. They would have liked fresh fruits and tender chickens.

"It is customary with us, when giving presents from the Emperor," the interpreter explained, "to include a certain quantity of rice."

While Perry and his officers were wondering what to do with so much rice and where to stow it on shipboard, twenty-five gigantic men tramped down the beach like so many elephants. The Americans guessed they were six feet tall and weighed at least three hundred pounds. They took off their purple and gold aprons and stood naked except for silk loin cloths.

Fat hung on their bull necks, on their chests and on their colossal arms and legs. Fat bulged their cheeks so that their eyes and noses were hardly visible. One of the biggest and fattest of the lot paraded in front of the Commodore—chest out, arms outstretched, fists clenched.

"Feel his muscles, sir," one of the treaty commissioners begged Perry. "Test him and feel how strong he is."

Perry felt the huge arm and found it a block of granite. He touched the neck and discovered that what seemed to be folds of fat were solid muscle. The Commodore shook his head in surprise. On all his travels he had never seen anything like this!

The giant grunted, as he was pleased to be admired. He and the other monster-men were professional wrestlers. The sport was known in Homer's day in ancient Greece. Over the centuries the Japanese had developed their own form of wrestling known as *sumo*. The contestants had to be as big as giants, as strong as bulls. For hundreds of years the princes of Japan had fed, trained and kept these wrestlers for their own amusement.

In *sumo* wrestling two men grapple with each other within a ring twelve feet in diameter. The loser is the man who lets any part of his body except his feet touch the ground, or who lets his feet be forced outside the circle.

Before the exhibition match Perry had to watch the wrestlers show their strength. At a word of command the twenty-five giants picked up the 140-pound rice bags, two at a time, and began carrying them to the water's edge. One of them took a sack between his teeth. Another, grabbing a rice bag in his colossal arms, somersaulted down the beach with it.

Now Perry and his officers took their seats to watch the wrestling match from a grandstand just outside the treaty house. Two by two the wrestlers walked slowly into the ring. Following the rules and traditions of *sumo*, the contestants crouched low, watched each other and waited for an opening. As they waited, they stamped the ground heavily like impatient horses, rubbed dirt between their palms and then threw it over their shoulders.

At the same instant the two giants heaved their bodies at each other and collided with a shock that would have stunned an ox. They locked their gorilla arms around each other, each trying to force the other out of the circle or to the ground. There was little movement in this clinch, but Perry could see the bulging of muscles and the reddening of necks and faces.

All of a sudden one of the wrestlers toppled heavily to the ground. He was helped to his feet and out of the ring. The first contest was over.

Next came a test of brute strength and stamina. One of the giants stood in the ring, bent forward, put one leg out to steady himself and lowered his head. Another wrestler rushed into the ring, bellowing like a bull. With his head lowered and thrust forward, he lunged at his opponent's lowered head. The defender took the shock without budging. But blood streamed down his face from his bruised forehead.

Again and again the same man attacked, the other resisted. Blood smeared their faces and great welts

swelled their chests as they banged their huge bodies
against each other.

The Americans were not impressed with the strength
of these athletes. Spalding of the *Mississippi* thought
American boxing champions "could no doubt whale
them with little difficulty." McCauley, now the acting
master of the *Powhatan,* said that "any wrestler I
have seen of half the muscle would have laughed at
them." The Commodore himself thought it was a
"brutal performance."

To most of the Americans it was "disgusting" as
well, although in the United States of those days prize
fighters used to batter each other into a bloody pulp
with bare fists. The visitors were glad when the show
was over. As Perry strode down the beach with the
Japanese commissioners, he felt he had escaped from
a stuffy room into fresh, clean air. He thought again
that America was far more civilized, more "enlight-
ened," than Japan.

Perry had planned to put the hospitality contest on
a higher plane—and to win it on American ground.
He would give a great feast for the Japanese on his
flagship. The moment had come. The discussions in
the treaty house were going well. The success of his
mission was in sight.

Before embarking for his flagship, the Commodore
invited Hayashi to come aboard in three days.

"Bring the other commissioners, the interpreters
and assistants with you," the Commodore said, think-

ing that the party might be as big as twenty. "How many will they be?"

Hayashi thought for a moment and consulted his colleagues.

"We shall be seventy," was his bland reply—"not including porters!"

17. Minstrels Shake Their Shoes

The next three days proved that Perry could have excelled as a banquet manager if he had not chosen a career in the Navy. His feast for the Japanese was going to be splendid and memorable. In his methodical way he thought of everything—the salutes, the food and wine, the seating arrangement, the after-dinner entertainment.

For this occasion the Commodore had reserved live bullocks, sheep and chickens. Now he ordered them slaughtered and cooked. Orders streamed in endless succession out of his secluded cabin on the *Powhatan*. His former flagship, the *Susquehanna*, had steamed away to Shanghai on an official mission, but the *Powhatan* would do just as well.

Although the new flagship was a third narrower than the old, its quarter-deck made a magnificent banquet hall. Perry knew that the five commissioners, as representatives of the Shogun, would resent sitting at the same table with their underlings. For that matter the Commodore himself seldom ate his meals with anyone except his captains, his son and secretary, Lieutenant Oliver Hazard Perry, and his other personal aides.

In Perry's cabin, therefore, a princely table was set for the Commodore, his ships' captains and the five Japanese commissioners and their interpreters. On the 45-foot-wide deck the other Americans and Japanese would sit at long tables under a huge awning.

The feast day was windy and squally. The American launches pitched and rolled as they brought the Japanese dignitaries out from shore. Many of the Japanese were queasy from the motion by the time they came aboard. As they clambered unsteadily aboard the flagship, they saw the black-and-white striped flag of their Shogun being run up the mast. Soon it was snapping in the brisk March wind.

To give Japanese stomachs a little time to settle, the Americans showed their visitors how one of the black ships worked. It was the first time Hayashi and his fellow commissioners had been aboard. A howitzer in the bow was fired off repeatedly for their amusement. The engines were started in their honor, and all 2,812 tons of the *Powhatan* shuddered and shook as the huge paddle wheels began revolving.

Soon it was time for dinner. The five commissioners, Hayashi leading them, retired to the Commodore's cabin. The rest of the visitors trooped to the quarterdeck and took their places at three long tables under the awnings.

Perry had thoughtfully placed American officers and interpreters at each table, one American for every four Japanese. A band perched on the roof of the wheelhouse played as the visitors sat down in curve-backed wooden chairs. Chairs were almost unknown in Japan, where everyone squatted cross-legged on the floor.

The tables were loaded with beef, lamb and poultry, with fish, vegetables and fruits, and with ample supplies of fine wines. Perry detested any drink stronger than wine; he used to lecture his crews on the evils of drunkenness. He also disliked tobacco. Sometimes, after dinner with friends, he would sit with an unlighted cigar clamped between his teeth. He did it only to be sociable.

This time his own likes and dislikes didn't matter.

Perry had learned on his earlier visit that most of the
Japanese liked strong Western drinks. More important,
strong drinks melted their stiffness and made them
talk more freely.

Hayashi was careful not to lose his dignity by eating or drinking too much. The other Japanese stowed
away so much, and so quickly, that the Americans
were amazed.

In no particular order they sampled all the dishes
that were spread out before them. What did it matter? Everything went down at once: a mouthful of
roast beef, then a mouthful of fish; a swallow of soup,
then one of syrup; fruit and fowl, pickles and pre-
serves, everything mixed happily together.

One American officer handed a Japanese neighbor
a mixture of ketchup and vinegar in a wine glass, to
see what would happen. He swallowed it and seemed
none the worse.

The Japanese washed down their unfamiliar food
with a cascade of wine and liquor. The mess-boys
busily refilled glasses with champagne. The Japanese
showed special fondness for maraschino, a sweet and
powerful brandy made of cherries; they drank un-
numbered glasses of it.

The party on deck soon became uproarious. Americans and Japanese jumped up to propose toasts to
the two countries, to American and Japanese women,
to the squadron. One Japanese got to his feet, a little
unsteadily, and proposed a toast to "Japan and Cali-

fornia: may they be united by steam!" Soon Japanese voices could be heard far above the brisk and cheerful rhythm of the band.

When everyone had eaten and drunk to the limit of his capacity, and beyond it, the Japanese guests pulled long paper handkerchiefs from inside their robes. They wrapped each piece of left-over food in the paper: a slice of beef, a piece of pie, a leg of chicken, the entire contents of a salt cellar. They stowed the packages away in their baggy, loose-flowing sleeves.

The Japanese were following the polite custom of their country—to take home unused food rather than to waste it. Besides, their families ashore might like to sample the American fare. Who could blame them for taking it?

The deep voice of the Commodore cut through the noise like a foghorn:

"Gentlemen, we will now adjourn to hear the minstrels!"

The interpreter had a hard time translating the word "minstrels" into Japanese. Old Japan had known wandering ballad singers and traveling troupes of clowns. But nothing in their experience had prepared the Japanese for what they were now to see on the deck of the *Powhatan*.

What the Commodore had provided for them was, of course, an old-fashioned minstrel show of black-faced comedians. The sailors had written the show, had rehearsed it, had blacked their faces with burnt cork. Now, with banjos and tambourines, nine of them trotted out onto an improvised stage.

The Japanese, sitting in places of honor in the front row, murmured with surprise. They had never seen such woolly heads, such huge white shirt collars, such charcoal-black faces and such crazy-patterned black and yellow jackets.

"Yah-yah, Sambo, how you be?" Mr. Bones asked Mr. Sambo. Sambo answered by knocking his tambourine into Bones's face. The polite Japanese almost choked trying to suppress their laughs. Soon they were guffawing as loudly as the Americans.

Even Prince Hayashi shook his stately sides with laughter. They could not understand the jokes, but they responded to the common language of slapstick as well as anyone.

The show ended at sunset. It was time for the Japanese to leave, but some had had too much wine and stronger drink. The oldest of the five commissioners was so tipsy that he threw his arms around Perry's neck. He squeezed so hard that he crushed a pair of new epaulets on the Commodore's broad shoulders.

Again and again he assured Perry, in fervent Japanese, "Japan and America, all the same heart!"

The Commodore shook himself loose and asked for the words to be translated. He overheard someone say:

"I don't think the Commodore will stand for *that!*"

"Oh," said Perry, "if he will only sign the treaty he may *kiss* me!"

The Japanese staggered to his boat, held up by some of his steadier companions, while a parting salute of seventeen guns boomed from the *Saratoga*. When all the visitors were safely ashore, Perry paced the deck thoughtfully in the twilight.

He hoped the revelry would make the Japanese more friendly and more willing to sign a treaty. The next few days would tell whether the Commodore's efforts as a banquet manager had been worth-while.

18. The Treaty at Last!

The mixture of so many strange foods and liquors had the result you might have expected. When Perry went ashore the next morning to continue the treaty talks, all the Japanese except Hayashi looked and behaved as if they had splitting headaches.

They didn't feel well, and they didn't even try to be agreeable. They argued, twisted, squirmed and stalled over every tiny point of the proposed treaty.

The Japanese commissioners acted like an out-weighed football team defending its own goal line. They knew that Perry had all the weight on his side— the power of big guns that could smash their crowded cities into pulp.

Someday, perhaps, their country would make and use the weapons Perry had shown them. Then she could meet the threats of the foreign "barbarians" on equal terms. For the moment all the Japanese could do was to dig their toes in, delay as much as possible and yield only after endless haggling.

One of the commissioners explained to Perry that Japanese did not usually come to the point as directly as Americans. He put it this way:

"Suppose, for example, that several Japanese met together and wanted to visit the American ships. One would say, 'It is a beautiful morning,' to which another would add, 'How pleasant it is!' Then a third would remark, 'There is not a wave to be seen upon the water.' At length a fourth would suggest, 'Come, let us go and see the ships.'"

Once or twice Perry hinted at the iron fist inside his velvet glove. He warned the Japanese that if they did not agree to help shipwrecked Americans, the United States would look upon them as cruel and inhuman.

"If your country becomes an enemy," he said, "we will exhaust our resources if necessary to wage war.

Our country has just had a war with a neighboring country, Mexico, and we even attacked and captured its capital. Circumstances may lead your country also into a similar plight."

This threatening language was not worthy of the Commodore, who said he had come as a friend. Hayashi, the chief Japanese commissioner, answered:

"Our government is not the inhumane thing you describe. We excel any other country in the importance we attach to human life. For this reason we have enjoyed peace for more than three hundred years. If we were so inhumane as to consider human life cheaply, the state I have described would not have been possible."

If some American seamen had been treated harshly in past years, the Shogun's agent went on, it was because they had behaved badly on shore and violated Japanese laws. And if the United States truly valued human life, he said, it would not let its annoyance push it into war with Japan.

Against one of Perry's demands the Japanese stood like a stone wall. They refused to consider a full-fledged trade treaty of the kind the United States had signed with China a few years before. Hayashi said firmly that Japan did not need a trade treaty since it was content to do without the produce of foreign countries.

But on other matters the Commodore's gifts and salutes and hospitality seemed to have done some good. The Japanese agreed to sign a more limited treaty, opening two ports to American ships. One was Shimoda, a little fishing port ninety miles southwest of Tokyo.

The other was the bigger port of Hakodate, far to the north, on the Japanese island of Hokkaido. Perry thought this was a real victory because Hokkaido was on the shortest route from northwestern United States to the China coast.

In the end Perry and the Japanese commissioners had reached agreement on enough terms to sign a treaty on March 31, 1854. It is known in the history books as the Treaty of Kanagawa, named for the big city nearest the treaty house. These were its main terms:

1. "There shall be a perfect, permanent, and universal peace, and a sincere and cordial amity, between the United States of America and the Empire of Japan, and between their people, without exception of persons and places.

2. "The port of Shimoda, in the principality of Idzu, and the port of Hakodate, in the principality of Matsumai, are granted by the Japanese as ports for the reception of American ships, where they can be supplied with wood, water, provisions, and coal, and other articles their necessities may require, as far as the Japanese have them.

3. "Whenever ships of the United States are thrown

or wrecked on the coast of Japan, the Japanese vessels will assist them, and carry their crews to Shimoda or Hakodate, and hand them over to their countrymen appointed to receive them.

4. "Those shipwrecked persons and other citizens of the United States shall be as free as in other countries, and not subjected to confinement, but shall be amenable to just laws.

5. "Shipwrecked men, and other citizens of the United States, temporarily living at Shimoda and Hakodate, shall not be subject to such restrictions and confinement as the Dutch and Chinese are at Nagasaki. They shall be free at Shimoda to go where they please within the limits of seven Japanese miles, and at Hakodate within limits to be defined after the visit of the United States squadron to that place.

6. "It is agreed that if, at any future day, the Government of Japan shall grant to any other nation or nations privileges and advantages which are not herein granted to the United States and the citizens thereof, the same privileges and advantages shall be granted likewise to the United States and to the citizens thereof without any consultation or delay.

7. "Ships of the United States shall be permitted to visit no other ports in Japan but Shimoda and Hakodate, unless in distress or forced by stress of weather.

8. "There shall be appointed by the Government of the United States consuls or agents to reside in Shi-

moda at any time eighteen months after the signing of the treaty; provided that either of the two governments deem such arrangement necessary."

These terms gave less than Perry had hoped for. He had asked for five ports and he got two. The two he got were by no means the best in Japan. Shimoda, a narrow harbor with a dangerous rock in the middle of it, was off the main trade routes. Hakodate, in the north, was fog-bound for most of the year.

All the same, the old Commodore was overjoyed. He had persuaded the Japanese to open their tightly shut door by just a crack. No other country had been able to do this for more than two hundred years. Perry was confident that other Americans would be able to push the door open further in the years to come.

As soon as the treaty had been signed, the Commodore gave an American flag as a final gift to Hayashi.

"This is the highest expression of national courtesy and friendship I can offer you," Perry said.

Hayashi, always careful not to show his feelings, simply answered:

"You are very kind."

Since the Japanese were the hosts, it was their turn to offer Perry and his officers a Japanese-style feast. The Americans sampled thick soup with fish in it; broiled crayfish, something like a small crab; pieces of fried fish, boiled shrimps, tiny candies and wafer-thin cakes. The Americans were hungry when the meal of little tidbits ended. Perry reckoned he had given the Japanese twenty times as much food at his feast aboard the *Powhatan*.

But the Commodore would have been happy on this day even if the Japanese had not fed him at all. He quickly ordered one of his sailing sloops, the *Saratoga*, to start for home, bearing the official copy of the treaty. This ship had been in Eastern waters for almost four years. Her men were tired and homesick almost beyond endurance.

When the ship sailed, with the other crews cheering and the bands playing "Home, Sweet Home," many of Perry's men felt lumps in their throats. They, too, had been away from home for many long months. They wished they could have been aboard the *Saratoga*.

19. "We Will Kill Ourselves!"

Now that the treaty was signed, barriers on both sides seemed to go down. Ordinary Japanese could show friendliness toward the Americans without getting scowls from Japanese officials. Perry allowed Japanese workers to visit the American ships. He found them intrigued by everything they saw, especially by Western clothing.

The Commodore reported later that the Japanese had tried eagerly to get samples of American uniforms, "and showed a peculiar passion for buttons."

"They would again and again ask for a button," the report said, "and when presented with the cheap gift, they stowed it away as if it were of the greatest value."

The reason, of course, was that the Japanese people used only sashes and ribbons to tie their kimonos and robes together.

The American sailors, too, were freed from ship-to-shore restrictions. Until the treaty had been signed, only the officers on Perry's staff and a few specialists like Dr. Morrow, the farm expert, had been allowed to stroll into the countryside.

At last the sailors could wander a few miles from Yokohama harbor. They could discover the beauty of the scenery, the neatness of the villages, the skillful cultivation of the tiny fields, the courtesy and politeness of the people.

On the first warm day of spring the Commodore himself shed some of his official dignity. He decided that he, too, would like a long walk ashore. He marveled at camellia bushes forty feet high, with red and white flowers in full bloom. Plum trees had blossomed, and new leaves had come out on the trees that were bare when the squadron had arrived two months earlier.

One thing annoyed Perry as he paced along,

flanked by his own officers and by Japanese officials and interpreters. As he approached the first village, he noticed that a Japanese messenger hurried ahead, shooing women and children into the houses. Perry turned to a Japanese official with that look of anger which his sailors feared.

"You should not have ordered the women out of the way," he said sternly. "I want to see as much as possible of the people. I want to learn all I can about them."

His orders were obeyed. At the second village everyone crowded around the big American "Admiral," so much taller, stouter and more bushy-haired than most of the Japanese. The mayor of the village invited Perry into his house for tea. The mayor's wife and sister bustled about in bare feet. They brought tea in tiny cups, cake, candy, and *sake*, the strong rice wine of Japan.

In serving the Commodore, they dropped to their knees, as Japanese waitresses do to this day. They kept bowing their heads, like bobbing dolls, and smiled at the Commodore although they could not understand a word he said.

As a final sign of hospitality the mayor's wife brought her eight-month-old baby son into the room for Perry to admire. The baby had a dirty face and looked untidy. When the Commodore gave him a piece of candy, the eight-month-old solemnly bowed his shaven head.

The mayor's wife brought her baby son into the room

Truly, Perry thought, these are the most polite people on earth—even their babies!

Not satisfied with his glimpse of ordinary Japanese life, the Commodore went back to his ship determined to see one sight no Westerner had seen. He wanted to take a look at the forbidden city of Tokyo before sailing away. The Japanese would not let him go into the city itself; very well, he would order his ships up the bay and anchor them within sight of the great capital.

The order to move produced something like panic among the Japanese officials. As the *Powhatan's* funnel began spouting black smoke, interpreters rowed frantically out to the ship and pleaded with Perry not to go nearer the city.

"Your life will be in danger, sir," they warned, "and the lives of all the commissioners too. If you anchor off the city, we will be dishonored, and all of us will have to perform *hara-kiri.*"

Hara-kiri, which means "happy despatch," was a ceremonial form of suicide in Japan. If a soldier lost a battle, or showed cowardice, or displeased his lord and master, he would slit his belly open with a dagger. A friend standing alongside would then swing a sharp sword and cut off the suicide's head.

Perry knew of this ancient custom; he had heard estimates that about four hundred Japanese killed themselves each year by *hara-kiri.*

The distracted interpreters explained that there

might be riots in Tokyo if the ships anchored close. The Shogun himself might be in danger, and he would surely regard the anchoring of the ships as an insult.

"The instant an anchor is gone," said one of the interpreters, "we will kill ourselves even though we happen to be in the Commodore's cabin!"

Not wanting to be responsible for mass suicides, Perry said he would bring his ships within sight of Tokyo without anchoring. He asked the interpreters to stay on board while the ships steamed toward the city. They stayed, but looked sick and miserable.

A fog prevented the Americans from seeing Tokyo clearly. As the ships glided cautiously nearer, their crews managed to discern the outlines of houses thickly crowded together. Most of them had low peaked roofs of the kind Perry and his men had seen in the villages around Yokohama. Half-finished stockades and forts suggested that the Japanese had started to strengthen their defenses, but had changed their minds about the time of Perry's second arrival.

The ships turned around and steamed slowly back to their anchorage. The interpreters, vastly relieved, did not rip their insides out. Instead they stayed for a meal and drinks with Perry and his officers. The Commodore was in a satisfied mood; he had at least had a look at the huge, hidden capital where the Shogun lived.

Now his mission was nearly over. His ships had

been in Tokyo Bay more than two months, and it was time to go. Their next assignment was to visit Shimoda, the nearer of the two treaty ports.

Four of the sailing ships went on ahead, and surveyed the shores of Tokyo Bay as they passed. Later the *Mississippi* and the *Powhatan,* with the Commodore aboard the latter, steamed for twelve hours down the coast until they reached the steeply terraced hillsides and the harbor of Shimoda. Here the squadron anchored for twenty-five days. They were to be the pleasantest days of the entire visit to Japan.

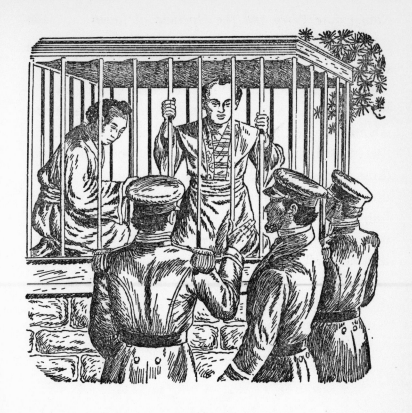

20. "When a Hero Fails . . ."

The sun was shining brightly, the sea was a sparkling blue, when a rowboat from the *Mississippi* landed an American officer on the beach near Shimoda. The officer was Spalding, the clerk of the *Mississippi*. He had made an appointment to meet Morrow, the farm expert, and Samuel Wells Williams, the interpreter, for a stroll into the countryside.

It was a perfect late April morning. The waves slapped rhythmically against the shore. On the white sands a cluster of farm villagers stood staring at the black hull of the warship out at sea. They watched the blue-coated foreigner step ashore.

As Spalding stood waiting for his companions, two sallow-faced Japanese walked up to him, bent over, grasped their knees in salutation and said what sounded to him like "Eh!" He could see by the way they were dressed that they were educated men, and gentlemen. They were wearing rich brocade trousers, in the baggy Japanese fashion. The handles of their short and long swords were decorated with charms.

Something desperately urgent was on their minds. Otherwise they would not have dared to defy the laws of their country by speaking to the foreigner.

They began by talking of unimportant things. They pointed to the warship, tried unsuccessfully to pronounce its name and then pretended to examine the chain of Spalding's watch. As one of them held the chain he suddenly slipped an envelope into Spalding's vest. The officer tried to pull it out, but the Japanese gently pulled his hand back.

Both Japanese looked around anxiously to see if anyone had noticed. With their eyes rather than words, for they could speak no English, they begged Spalding to keep the letter a secret and to say no more. At this moment two local officials came through the sand to where the group was standing. The Japanese in their brocades bowed ceremoniously and walked away in the opposite direction.

Spalding kept the letter and for a time dismissed it from his mind. His friends, the farm expert and the interpreter, soon arrived on shore, and the three Americans set off on an all-day walk into the hilly country behind Shimoda.

They watched farmers at work, they inspected temples and wayside shrines. Late in the afternoon they rested on the steps of a temple and ate a picnic lunch they had brought from the ship. Suddenly Spalding remembered the letter he still carried in his vest.

"Williams," he said, "a couple of Japanese gave me this while I was waiting for you this morning. I wonder if you'd read it and tell me what it's about."

Williams opened the envelope, read the Japanese characters and said, "This is important. I think the Commodore ought to see it."

The heading of the letter described it as "a secret communication for the American men-of-war ships." The letter was a plea to Perry to take the two Japanese to America so they could learn about the Western world for the benefit of their country.

That night, while the *Mississippi's* crew were asleep in their hammocks below, the officer on watch duty heard someone whispering, "American! American!"

from the top of the gangway. Before he could investigate further, two young Japanese jumped onto the darkened deck.

They pointed to their rowboat, which they had tied to the ship's side, and held up their hands to show the blisters on them, as if to say they were tired from long rowing. By sign language they indicated that they wanted to set their rowboat adrift and stay on the warship. This, of course, was against the Commodore's orders.

There was nothing to do but awaken Williams, the interpreter, who could translate from the Japanese. Williams discovered at once that these were the same Japanese who had handed the secret letter to Spalding. Seeking instructions, he hurried to Perry's cabin.

"What do they want?" Perry asked sleepily.

"They want to stay aboard, sir," was the answer.

"They can't do that unless they get the permission of their government," the Commodore ruled.

When Williams relayed the message, the two men showed clearly that they were afraid. They pleaded that they would be beheaded if they returned to shore, because they had violated their country's laws by trying to go abroad. But Williams had to be stony-hearted on Perry's orders. He ordered a boat to put the two men ashore in the dead of night, at a point where they might avoid being caught.

With one last imploring look the two men clambered over the side into the darkness.

A few days later a group of officers strolling on the outskirts of Shimoda, near the city prison, were horrified to find the two young Japanese in a barred cage. The cage measured no more than six feet long and wide, and was not high enough for them to stand in. As the prisoners saw the Americans approaching, they scribbled a note on a piece of board and slipped it through the bars. It said:

"When a hero fails in his purpose, his acts are then regarded as those of a villain and a robber. In public we have been seized and pinioned and caged for many days. It must now be seen whether a hero will prove himself to be one indeed.

"We wished to make the circuit of the five great continents. This was our hearts' wish for a long time. Suddenly our plans are defeated, and we find ourselves in a half-sized house where eating, resting, sitting and sleeping are difficult. How can we find our exit from this place?

"Weeping, we seem as fools; laughing, as rogues. Alas! for us; silent we can only be." The letter was signed "Yoshida Shoin."

When the Commodore heard what had happened to the visitors, he sent his flag lieutenant to shore in the hope of getting them out of their cage. The officer found the cage empty, and was told that the two captives had been hustled off to Tokyo. The authorities sent word to Perry that, whatever happened to them, they would not be beheaded for what they had done.

But the two men were kept in close confinement. Yoshida Shoin was released after a year; his friend died in prison. Yoshida became a writer and schoolteacher, and some of his pupils were to become famous political leaders who fought and finally overthrew the dictatorship in later years.

He came to a tragic end. In 1858 he was arrested and put in jail for plotting the murder of a high official. Three months later Yoshida Shoin knelt in the prison courtyard; the executioner's bright sword flashed, and the life of this restless Japanese patriot came to a sudden end.

Perry never knew the fate of the man who had tried to discover the world outside Japan. But in the brief meeting with Yoshida and his companion, the Americans caught still another glimpse of Japan's cruel laws and of the yearning for freedom that was stirring within the Japanese people.

21. A Nest of Spies

Wherever the Americans walked on shore during their first days in Shimoda, they were shadowed, spied upon and pestered by agents of the police.

Sometimes the Americans tried to shake off the spies by out-walking them. Edward McCauley of the *Powhatan*, a tall and rangy Philadelphian, knew that he could cover more ground with every step than could the short-legged Japanese. He and three friends decided to walk at top speed and see what would happen.

The young Japanese who had been assigned to follow them could not keep up. Soon he was shouting at them, "Na!" "Ney!" "No!" "American!" "Noah!"— slipping and stumbling over every ditch and gulley.

"He still followed, chattering like a beaten monkey," McCauley wrote in his diary. "I never walked so fast for so long a time in my life. We walked at that pace for three hours, no less than ten miles.

"Finally we threw him into a paroxysm of anguish by making a dash at a high hill. His woebegone appearance made us lie down and kick with laughter, which must have spoiled his taste for Yankee-tracking ever afterward. When he got up to us, he implored us to wait while he cooled himself, which he did by stripping and getting a peasant to rub him down."

The Commodore saw nothing funny in all this snooping and spying. The new treaty had given Americans the right to walk freely within seven miles of the rock in Shimoda harbor. Clearly the Japanese were breaking the agreement they had signed. Perry sent an angry message to the police chief of Shimoda.

"If these annoyances to our men continue," he wrote, "I shall sail to Tokyo with my whole squadron and demand an explanation."

". . . the terraced fields high up on the hillsides"

The Commodore was kept busy sending protests to the Japanese. One evening three of his officers were stranded in Shimoda after a day on shore. It was too late for them to go back to their ships, and they decided to sleep in the lodging quarters of a Buddhist temple. The Japanese had agreed that these rooms could be used as a rest house for the Americans.

But in the middle of the night a troop of soldiers stormed into the temple, pulled the sleeping Americans to their feet and ordered them back to their ships at once.

The Americans grabbed their revolvers and pointed them at the soldiers. Luckily they did not shoot. The Japanese let them spend the night in the temple, but posted a guard outside. Once more the angry Commodore had to send officers to argue with the chief of police, to make sure that such a thing would not happen again.

Perry complained, too, that the Japanese were ordering villagers to get off the streets and close up their houses whenever Americans on shore leave came within sight. This, again, was contrary to the treaty. You would have thought, from Japanese behavior at Shimoda, that the Americans were carriers of disease germs. The Japanese agreed at last not to shadow the Americans, not to hustle the villagers out of sight, and to treat the visitors as friends.

Once they were rid of restrictions, the Americans

had a happy time at Shimoda. They found Japanese girls bright and attractive, but they thought married women made themselves disgusting by blackening and filing their teeth. They could not get used to the sight of women doing the heaviest manual work.

"I saw a woman carrying a bundle that would have been weight enough to founder a man and a boy," McCauley noted in his diary. "I saw a woman carrying water enough for twenty men and twenty boys. I saw a woman pounding rice with a big mallet that would have broken the heart of twenty men and any number of boys."

As for Japanese children, McCauley thought they were "brats" who behaved much like children anywhere else in the world: "squalling, tumbling, fretting and making themselves universally unpleasant." But, he noticed, "they were clean, well scrubbed, and in fact, holystoned, inasmuch as sand does duty for soap" in Japanese households.

Now the Americans were free to shop for silks and curios to bring to their sweethearts and families at home. As they strolled in the hills beyond Shimoda, past rushing brooks and toylike farmhouses, they marveled at the terraced fields high up on the hillsides. Some of these Americans had visited Italy and other countries where terracing was common. But they had never seen such perfect workmanship as on the stone banks of these Japanese terraces. The terraces had been built with sweat and labor centuries ago, and still produced a crop of underwater rice in the summer and barley or wheat in the winter.

During their stay of almost a month at Shimoda, Perry's men surveyed every foot of the harbor. Now it was time to inspect Hakodate, the second of the treaty ports. The Commodore ordered three of his sailing ships to start ahead of him. A day later the two steamers, with Perry's broad pennant flying from the *Powhatan,* chugged out of the harbor.

Off to the northwest the crews could see the snowy cap of Mount Fuji. The helmsmen steered close to an island where a volcano was belching steam and smoke. Then they shifted their course northward, onto the heaving ocean, bound for unknown shores once more.

22. Northward, Southward—and Home!

The ships struggled northward on a stormy, rain-soaked voyage of 600 miles. Their goal was Hakodate, on the southern tip of the bleak, austere island of Hokkaido.

In those days Hokkaido was like a foreign country to most Japanese, although one of their princes ruled it. It was a cold frontier land of forests, bears and

147

volcanoes. The island is about the same size as the state of Maine, and has the same kind of climate—often foggy along the coast in the summer, deep in snow in the winter.

As for Hakodate, which the Japanese pronounce in four syllables, "Hak-ko-dat-te," the American sailors promptly nicknamed it "Hack Your Daddy"! They found it a clean but dreary city. A single mountain towering above it reminded old-timers on the squadron of Gibraltar and Cape Town.

The arrival of Perry's ships, apparently without notice, produced a panic in the city. You would have thought that they were space ships from Mars. Women and children hurried out of the town first. The men followed with pack horses laden with household goods.

For several days Perry's men could see the pack trains winding away over a long sandy plain, like camel caravans in the desert.

The city had not yet heard of the treaty signed at Yokohama. The people thought the Americans had come as enemies to avenge the ill-treatment of American seamen who had been wrecked on Hokkaido's coast a few years before. The Commodore stopped the panic by showing the officials a copy of the treaty which had opened Hakodate to American ships.

As usual Perry ordered his men to survey the harbor and its surroundings. He sent one of his armed

store ships, the *Southampton,* into Volcano Bay, which
was ringed by several volcanoes, two of them smok-
ing at the time. There the sailors found some of the
true curiosities of Hokkaido.

These were the Ainus, or, as they were called in
Perry's day, the "hairy Kuriles," the primitive people
who were living in Japan before the ancestors of the
present-day Japanese arrived.

In the seventeenth century there were about
200,000 of these stocky, long-haired people living
on Hokkaido. By Perry's day the number had shrunk
to between 20,000 and 30,000 chiefly because a small-
pox epidemic had almost wiped them out a century
before.

The *Southampton's* commander described them
as only about five feet tall, "but well-proportioned,
with intelligent features." He noted their "very black,
coarse hair."

It was not only the hair that made the Ainus so
conspicuous among the smooth-skinned Japanese. The
Ainu eyes and skin showed that they were related to a
white race, in contrast to the yellow, almond-eyed Japanese.

Probably they came to the Japanese islands from
nearby Manchuria in prehistoric times. They were
fishermen and bear-hunters, living off the game they
could find in their dark, damp forests. The early Japanese, pushing up from the south, drove them north-

ward, much as our own early American settlers drove the Indians into smaller and smaller areas in the West and North.

The most faithful friends of these primitive people were their Ainu dogs, a wolfish breed something like the "huskies" of the Eskimos. Perry sent three of these dogs all the way back to America with the other gifts and treasures he had acquired in Japan.

But the Commodore had not come all the way to Hokkaido just to see Ainus or Ainu dogs. He wanted Hakodate opened up at once to American ships, as the treaty provided. This port, he thought, would be more useful than Shimoda, because it was near the routes of American whaling ships in the north Pacific.

More important still, just across the narrow Sea of Japan was Russian territory. The Russians, who then owned Alaska, had their eyes on Hokkaido. Perry distrusted the Russians, and was determined that American ships should get the use of Hakodate ahead of them.

As usual the Commodore ran into exasperating delays. But he was patient and persistent. Before long the Japanese agreed to let the Americans land, and opened a bazaar or market place for them.

This time not all of the Americans behaved as well as at Yokohama or Shimoda. Some of the officers, seeing swords on display in front of a shop, forced the shopkeeper to sell them, although it was against the laws of Japan.

McCauley wrote in his diary that an American engineer wanted to buy a pack of Japanese cards (long strips of pasteboard with curlicues on them) which the shopkeeper would not sell. A Japanese policeman with two swords stamped into the shop and ordered the Americans to put the cards down.

The engineer took off his high crowned hat and mashed it down on the policeman's head. Then, grabbing the policeman by the shoulders, he turned him round and kicked him in the seat of his pants, out of the shop and across the street.

"This was done to the great amusement of the shopmen and bystanders," McCauley wrote. "After this feat, the American engineer could get anything he wanted, and has the best collection of lacquer ware on board."

Perry himself did not get a completely satisfactory agreement with the Japanese on Hokkaido. He left some of the details to be worked out in a final meeting at Shimoda, where the five commissioners, headed by Hayashi, were waiting for him.

All the familiar Japanese faces from Tokyo Bay were there—except one. Kayama, the so-called Governor, the official welcomer and friend at the time of the first landing, was missing. When the Americans asked about him, the Japanese were oddly silent.

Kayama, it seemed, was in disgrace with his own government, perhaps because he had been too friendly to the foreigners. The Americans never saw him again.

The Shimoda conference was Perry's last chance in Japan to stage a military show. With his love of uniformed pageantry—of "boom-a-laddying," as one of his officers called it—he again sent his marines and bands ashore in full dress. This time he ordered them to take along a battery of artillery. It was a silly order, with no other purpose than to show off American strength.

While Perry was talking to the commissioners, the bandsmen gave a concert for the people of Shimoda in a temple courtyard. Showing what was on their minds, they played "Home, Sweet Home." Most of them would soon be on their way.

The Commodore and the Japanese drew up a set of rules which amounted to an addition to the treaty. When the work had ended, the Japanese commissioners announced that they were giving Perry a special gift to take home.

It was a block of Japanese stone for the Washington Monument, which was rising slowly in the American capital. This stone, Hayashi said, was a tribute from Japan to the great father of the American Republic.

Among the many other presents Perry took home

were three Japanese pugdogs. On shipboard the yapping pets found a home on the poop deck in what was beginning to look, smell and sound like a little zoo. About twenty Ainu dogs added to the general din, along with tailless Japanese cats, long-tailed Japanese roosters, and, swinging in cages, pheasants, mandarin ducks and songbirds—all bound for new homes in the United States.

The ships were ready to sail for home on June 25, 1854, more than four months after their chilly arrival in Tokyo Bay. Perry and his crews were the last Americans to see Shimoda as it looked then. A few months later an underwater earthquake shook the floor of the sea. Five times it sucked the water of the harbor out to the ocean; five huge tidal waves, like walls of water, raced inland, crashed against the shore and swept away all but sixteen of Shimoda's houses.

A Russian warship happened to be in the harbor at the time. The convulsion of the water spun the warship completely around forty-three times in thirty minutes, and damaged it beyond repair.

Thousands raced up the hillsides as they saw the tidal waves coming. Hundreds failed to get to high ground in time and were drowned. When Captain Adams of the *Powhatan* revisited Shimoda after the earthquake, bringing the ratified copy of the treaty back from America, the town was a wreck. But the Japanese were already hammering and sawing away on new houses.

Perry's ships stopped at Okinawa, in the Ryukyu Islands, on the way home. In all his dealings with these islands Perry showed the worst side of his character. When he stopped there first, on his way to Japan, he advised the United States to annex Okinawa as a naval and coaling base. The government in Washington, wiser than the Commodore, refused. Between his first and second Japanese visits he stopped there again and threatened the local ruler in his efforts to get a coaling station there.

Now, on his final visit, he tried to frighten the people as well as the officials by sending a showy armed procession ashore. The Commodore behaved strangely, too, at a Sunday service on deck during this visit to Okinawa. A missionary preached a sermon in which he likened Perry to Jesus Christ, and compared his mission to Japan to Jesus' mission on earth. Perry listened without any apparent displeasure.

Maybe Perry had not heard the preacher. Maybe he was tired and thinking of his home and family. Months before, racked with rheumatism, he had written to the Secretary of the Navy asking to be relieved of his command at the end of his second visit to Japan. At Hong Kong he found a letter from Washington saying that he could come home on leave.

As he walked off the gangplank of the *Mississippi*

at Hong Kong, the sailors crowded the rigging and gave him three cheers. The tribute from these rough, simple sailors would linger in his memory on the long voyage home.

23. How Perry Shaped History

The Japan Expedition was ended. Perry had pierced a wall within which Japan had imprisoned herself for 216 years. In doing so, he changed the course of history.

Other naval commanders—Drake, Nelson or Nimitz, for example—shaped the future in a single battle. But Perry did it without firing a shot.

The Commodore's boldness brought a great new power into the modern world. Within three years of Perry's visit Britain, Russia and the Netherlands had made treaties of friendship opening Japanese ports to their ships.

Within four years Townsend Harris, the first American consul, obtained the first full-fledged trade treaty with Japan.

Within twenty years a modern railroad was carrying freight and passengers between Tokyo and Yokohama. It was the direct descendant of the circular track with its model train which Perry had given the Japanese on the shores of Tokyo Bay.

Japan quickly developed an ocean-going merchant marine, an efficient army and navy, and an industrial system which held its own with those of Britain and the United States. The Western world was amazed to see this island empire, so weak in Perry's day, shoot up like Jack's Beanstalk to the size and strength of a modern giant.

Perry was only partly responsible. His visit gave the final push which toppled the weak and decaying rule of the Shoguns. Japanese patriots, like Yoshida Shoin, had long been eager to open Japan's windows to the outer world. They wanted to use the science and skill of the West to make Japan strong.

The sight of Perry's ships proved to the Japanese, even to the Shogun himself, that their country could not survive behind closed doors. Pressure from many discontented groups forced the Shogun to resign in 1867. The Emperor came out of his godlike seclusion in Kyoto to become the ruler of Japan in fact as well as in name.

Known in history as the Emperor Meiji, he surrounded himself with brilliant and far-seeing advisers. They quickly adopted Western methods—not because they loved the West, but because they wanted to use its railroads, ships, factories, rifles and cannon to make Japan powerful.

If they had not moved fast, Japan might have become a colony of some armed and aggressive Western nation. While the European powers were busy with wars and conquests elsewhere, Japan grew strong enough to stand on her own feet and face the West on equal terms.

This is one reason why intelligent Japanese now honor Perry as the man who started their country on the road to fifty years of dazzling progress.

If there had been a United Nations in Perry's day —if there had been a Charter pledging nations not to use or threaten force—the Japan Expedition would have been regarded as a threat to world peace. Japan or some other nation could have brought the threat before the Security Council, and the United States would have been in the wrong. There cannot be the slightest doubt about it.

For although Perry did not use force, he certainly

threatened to use it against the Japanese. Didn't he
say, repeatedly, that he would land his men and
march them to the Japanese capital if necessary to
get the President's letter delivered? Didn't he threaten
the Japanese by bringing back a bigger, more powerful squadron on his second visit than on his first?

Moreover, the Commodore and most of his men
had contempt for the Japanese and their ancient
civilization. The Americans were "culture-bound"—
that is, they considered Japan *inferior* simply because
it was *different*.

Again and again Perry's official report and his officers' diaries remarked that everything American was
better and nobler than anything Japanese. The chief
clerk of the *Mississippi* wrote that Japanese songs
were a mixture of "the half wail, half-vocal screech
of the Chinese, a boy dragging a stick over a picket
fence, and a severe asthma."

According to the visitors, their wrestling matches
were "disgusting," their food was miserable, they
were deceitful and treacherous, and so on. To most
of the Americans it made no difference that Japan had
had a splendid and radiant art when America was
still a wilderness. The Americans honestly believed
they were bringing the blessings of civilization to a
backward, heathen people.

Yet you have to judge Perry against the background of his own time, not of ours. It was the prac-

tice of powerful European nations in the mid-nine-
teenth century to be arrogant and harsh toward
Asians.

Only ten years before Perry went to Japan, the
British fought a war against China and killed thousands of helpless people—for the right to sell opium
in China! The result was a series of treaties which
gave the British special rights in Chinese ports, as if
they were a superior race. The French were beginning the conquest of Indo-China, bombarding towns
and killing civilians. The Dutch and the British had
already grabbed the East Indies and India as colonies.

Perry had a chance to do the same when he came
knocking at the closed door of Japan. He thought
the door was made of iron; he found that it was made
of bamboo and paper. He could have pushed it by
force, but he and his government in Washington
were wise enough not to do so.

Instead he showed respect and courtesy toward the
Japanese. Compared with the bully-and-grab tactics
of his day, Perry's conduct in Japan was a model of
dignity, fairness and restraint. He did not try to annex an inch of Japanese soil for the United States.

Japan would have been opened anyway, even if
Perry had not gone there. Great Britain or Russia
surely would have done it someday. If any nation
was to open Japan by the threat of force, probably
it was fortunate that the United States did it. Although our government was thinking of its own self-

interest in sending Perry, its purpose was only to establish trade and friendship with Japan. It wanted Japan to be a good neighbor.

It was not Perry's fault that twentieth-century Japan became a fierce and dangerous enemy of the United States. The Japanese took a wrong turning about fifty years after Perry's visit. They modeled their constitution on that of Prussia, the most warlike of the German states. In the 1890's the Emperor's advisers ruled that the minister of war and the minister of navy must be a general and an admiral on active service.

From then on the army and the navy held the whip hand over the civilians in Japan's government. In 1894 Japan launched a war against China; one purpose was to show off Japanese power. In 1904 Japan fought and won a bloody, costly war against Russia which gave her control of Korea. In 1937 she attacked China and began seriously to plan the conquest of all of eastern Asia.

In 1941 she made war on the United States by bombing Pearl Harbor. Japan was defeated and almost ruined. World War II smashed her cities to heaps of rubble, destroyed her merchant fleet and navy, and wasted almost a quarter of all the wealth she had built up since Perry's time. Her leaders surrendered on the decks of the American battleship *Missouri* at almost the exact spot where Perry's squadron had anchored in Tokyo Bay.

Today thoughtful Japanese wish their country had continued on the course of peaceful progress that Perry started. They no longer look upon Perry's visit with shame. School children learn about it in their history books and regard Perry as a man who helped to save and revive their country.

In Japan as in the United States, the thick-set figure of the Commodore looms larger with the passing years. And his black ships, once so terrifying, are remembered as heralds of Japanese freedom.

24. The Commodore's Last Voyage

Perry came home as a civilian. He chose to make the long journey to America as an ordinary passenger on a British liner, and not as a Commodore aboard one of his own warships. He had had enough of Navy life for a time.

In the British colony of Hong Kong he packed away the uniforms and the gold braid he had worn in

Japan. It was a Navy regulation that he could not
wear them on foreign soil or on foreign ships in time
of peace. Instead he put on the dark clothes, the
high collar and flowing tie of a gentleman of the
1850's.

With his flag lieutenant as his only companion, he
sailed to India and Egypt aboard the British mail
steamer *Hindostan,* then one of the finest ships afloat.
In England he stopped in Liverpool to spend Christ-
mas with Nathaniel Hawthorne, then the United
States Consul in that gloomy seaport town. He had
met Hawthorne before going to Japan.

Hawthorne told friends that he found Perry "brisk,
gentlemanly, off-hand but not rough; unaffected and
sensible." The Commodore tried to persuade Hawthorne to write the official story of the Japan Expedition. But the famous author of *The Scarlet Letter*
decided that he could not tackle the job. Perry would
have to look elsewhere for someone to write his fab-
ulous story.

At Liverpool he climbed the gangplank of the
British passenger liner *Baltic.* Its graceful lines reminded him in many ways of his favorite warship,
the *Mississippi.* Thirteen days later, on a cold, foggy
morning in January, 1855, he stepped onto the pier
in New York.

He was happy to be reunited with his wife and
grown-up children at Tarrytown, up the Hudson

from New York. His neighbor Washington Irving, who was then working on a life of George Washington, was there to welcome him and to listen to his stories of faraway Japan.

By now Perry was a hero to the merchants and ship-owners of New York and New England, and to all who cared deeply about the Navy. It seemed to the Commodore that life was a succession of receptions and dinners in his first months back at home. In Newport, Rhode Island, near where he was born, a big crowd welcomed him in front of the State House. The governor gave him a solid silver tray that weighed almost twenty pounds. It was a gift of the people of Rhode Island, paid for with money voted by the State Assembly.

The government in Washington had changed hands since Perry sailed for Japan. President Fillmore and the Whigs had been defeated by President Franklin Pierce and the Democrats. Pierce and his party paid little attention to the Commodore. They were not sure that the opening of Japan had any value to the United States. Still, Pierce's State Department asked Perry for advice on whom to appoint to diplomatic posts in the Far East.

Since Perry wanted his place in history, he gave much thought to the official report of his expedition. He wanted America and all the world to know what obstacles he had faced in Japan, how he had met them and what he had achieved. He finally persuaded the Reverend Francis Hawks, a southerner who was then the minister of his own St. Mark's Church in New York, to write the report. Perry took a room in Washington, and for a whole year worked with Dr. Hawks in writing and editing the story.

A grateful Congress voted $360,000 to finance the work, and gave Perry a bonus of $20,000 besides. The result was a set of three fat volumes, solemn and humorless like the Commodore himself, but also vivid, well arranged and accurate. The books had many colored pictures by artists whom Perry had taken to Japan with him. To the Congressmen and to their friends at home who got copies, these books gave the first up-to-date knowledge of Japan. Perry got a thousand sets himself and gave half of them to Dr. Hawks.

He was always in demand as a public speaker. He talked freely about world politics and more than once foresaw an eventual clash between America and Russia.

"If Russia possessed Japan," the Commodore said, "she would have an abundance of harbors, unrivaled in the world for excellency, and with her resources would control the commerce of the Pacific. It is not, therefore, the interest of any part of the commercial world that Russia should ever own Japan."

In one speech he predicted that America would extend her power to the eastern shores of Asia, and would come into a tremendous collision with Russia.

"Then," he said solemnly, "will be fought the mighty battle on which the world will look with breathless interest; for on its issue will depend the freedom or the slavery of the world. I think I see in the distance the giants that are growing up for that fierce and final encounter."

Among those "giants" he did not see Japan. He did not dream that Japan would rise, within a hundred years, to fight America in the most terrible of all oceanic wars.

Early in 1858 Perry was proud to be named commander of the American fleet in the Mediterranean. He liked the brilliant sun and warmth of the Mediterranean, where he had served as a young officer. But he never went.

On a bitter cold week end in March, 1858, his old enemy, rheumatism, stabbed him with pain as he sat in the library of his New York home. He died soon after midnight, at the age of sixty-four. Flags dropped to half-mast all over New York. The Commodore had sailed away on his last voyage.

Perry would have enjoyed his own funeral. Five hundred officers and men of the Seventh National Guard Regiment, New York's finest, turned up in their new blue uniforms to march in the parade.

A hundred marines marched slowly at the head of the procession, in the tall-hatted uniforms that had given such a martial look to Perry's landings in Japan. Old General Winfield Scott, the Mexican War hero whom Perry resembled in so many ways, was among the many important people who rode in carriages.

But the real stars of this solemn parade were fifty tough, hard-bitten men wearing the blue jackets and blue trousers of the United States Navy. These were men who had served with Perry on the Japan Expedition. Most of them had left the Navy and were working at other jobs in and around New York. When the news reached them that the Commodore had died, they bought or rented uniforms with their own money so that they could pay their final respects to their leader.

St. Mark's Church was filled for the funeral service. The old Commodore was buried in the churchyard, and the marines fired three volleys as a final salute over his grave.

Today, more than a hundred years after the Japan Expedition, Perry is remembered in the United States and in modern Japan. The United States Post Office brought out a special five-cent stamp in 1953 for the hundredth anniversary of his landing. At Shimoda, Uraga and Hakodate, the Japanese stage a festival almost every summer to commemorate the black ships which struck terror into their ancestors long ago.

The center of Perry observances in Japan is a granite monument, thirty-three feet high, at Kurihama. It stands in a sandy enclosure known as "Perry Park" at the exact spot where the Commodore delivered the letter from President Fillmore. An inscription in English says: "This monument commemorates the first arrival of Commodore Perry, Ambassador from the United States of America, who landed at this place July 14, 1853."

From Tokyo, the capital Perry never entered, to Kurihama beach, where he first stepped onto Japanese soil, it is an easy trip by fast electric train. A dusty road along the beach is lined with one-story tea houses and soft-drink stands. But the surroundings have not changed much since Perry was there.

At one end of the crescent beach is the bold headland behind which Perry's ships first anchored. At the other end the land rises in gentle slopes as green as Perry's Rhode Island in the summertime. On clear days you can catch a glimpse, as Perry did, of the white peak of Fuji against the deep blue sky.

Let your imagination go, and you will have no trouble at all in flitting backward a hundred years in time. Stand quietly, look carefully. Details of the scene will change. The road and the tea houses will disappear. The beach will come alive with scarlet pennons and brilliant flags. A thousand Japanese soldiers with flashing swords will be standing in the background.

Out on the blue water four black ships will be letting down their anchor chains. A proud figure of a man, in a tight-fitting blue and gold uniform, will step from a boat to the shore. And if you listen carefully, you will be able to hear the bands playing "Hail, Columbia!"

If You Want to Read More About Perry

Luckily there is a wealth of material about the Japan Expedition, written by men who were aboard Perry's ships. The most valuable source of information, of course, is the Commodore's official three-volume report.

The three volumes are out of print and hard to find. But a shortened version was published in 1953, on the hundredth anniversary of the first landing. This one-volume account, edited by Sidney Wallach, is easily available in public libraries.

Its title, like that of the original story, is *Narrative of the Expedition of an American Squadron to the China Seas and Japan.* When you read it, remember that Perry read the manuscript and edited every line of it.

Two other accounts written in Perry's day will reward you if you are willing to search for them in the bigger public libraries. One, *The Japan Expedition,* published in 1855, is by J. W. Spalding, the chief clerk of the *Mississippi* on both of Perry's visits to Japan. In small details it is not as accurate as the official story, but it has humor and liveliness that are missing in the *Narrative.*

The second major account, written and published in Perry's day, fills eight chapters of Bayard Taylor's *Visit to India, China and Japan.* It was published in 1855 and reprinted later in the collected edition of Taylor's writings.

Taylor was a traveler, author and poet who happened to be in China as a young newspaper correspondent when Perry arrived there on his way to Japan. Perry took him aboard, made him an officer, and later used Taylor's notes in the official *Narrative.* Taylor's book tells only of the first visit, whereas Spalding's describes both the first and second.

Two of Perry's officers kept secret journals which have been published in recent years. They should be easy to find in good libraries. One, *With Perry in Japan: the Diary of Edward Yorke McCauley,* was edited by Allan B. Cole and published in 1942. McCauley was only twenty-five when he sailed aboard the *Powhatan* for Japan. He lived to become a rear admiral.

The other is the journal of Dr. James Morrow, the South Carolina farm expert who visited Japan on the second voyage. Morrow's story, *A Scientist With Perry in Japan,* was also edited by Allan B. Cole and published in 1947.

The McCauley and Morrow stories are all the more valuable today because Perry never saw them. The old Commodore forbade his officers to write journals which he personally could not see and censor. He did not want criticisms of his own conduct to come from members of his expedition. So McCauley and Morrow kept their diaries to themselves, and the manuscripts were not discovered until decades afterward.

The best full-scale history of the Perry expedition is *Black Ships Off Japan* by Arthur Walworth, published in 1946. The standard biography of Perry is *The Great Commodore* by Edward M. Barrows, published in 1936. Less than half of this book deals with the Japan Expedition.

Perry took an official artist with him to paint and sketch the scenes of the landings and of Japan of a century ago. Most of these pictures appeared in the three big volumes of the official account. Many are reproduced in the Walworth book, and some of the best appeared in the *National Geographic Magazine* of July, 1953, with an article on "The Yankee Sailor Who Opened Japan." I thank the editors of the *National Geographic* for letting me use, in this book, some of the material which I originally wrote for their pages.

F.K.

Index

LANDMARK BOOKS

★

Have you read these World Landmarks?

★

CHECK THE LIST BELOW